Diagnostic Map: Measurement

What is the Diagnostic Map for Measurement?

How students currently think about measurement attributes and units will influence how they respond to the activities provided for them, and hence what they are able to learn from them. As students' thinking about measurement develops, it goes through a series of characteristic phases. Recognising these common patterns of thinking should help you to interpret students' responses to activities, to understand why they seem to be able to do some things and not others, and also why some students may be having difficulty in achieving certain outcomes while others are not. It should also help you to provide the challenges students need to move their thinking forward, to refine their half-formed ideas, to overcome any misconceptions they might have and hence to achieve the outcomes.

During the Emergent Phase

Students initially attend to overall appearance of size, recognising one thing as perceptually bigger than another and using comparative language in a fairly undifferentiated and absolute way (big/small) rather than to describe comparative size (bigger/smaller). Over time, they note that their communities distinguish between different forms of bigness (or size) and make relative judgments of size.

As a result, they begin to understand and use the everyday language of attributes and comparison used within their home and school environment, differentiating between attributes that are obviously perceptually different.

... of the Emergent phase, students typically:

- distinguish tallness, heaviness, fatness and how much things hold
- start to distinguish different forms of length and to use common contextual length distinctions; e.g. distinguish wide from tall
- use differentiated bipolar pairs to describe things; e.g. thin–fat, heavy–light, tall–short
- describe two or three obvious measurement attributes of the same thing; e.g. tall, thin and heavy
- describe something as having more or less of an attribute than something else, e.g. as being taller than or as being fatter than.

Mos
Qua
7 an

During the Matching and Comparing Phase

Students match in a conscious way in order to decide which is bigger by familiar readily perceived and distinguished attributes such as length, mass, capacity and time. They also repeat copies of objects, amounts and actions to decide how many fit (balance or match) a provided object or event.

As a result, they learn to directly compare things to decide which is longer, fatter, heavier, holds more or took longer. They also learn what people expect them to do in response to questions such as 'How long (tall, wide or heavy, much time, much does it hold)?' or when explicitly asked to measure something.

By the end of the Matching and Comparing phase, students typically:

- attempt to focus on a particular attribute to compare two things; e.g. how much the jar holds
- know that several things may be in different orders when compared by different attributes
- line up the base of two sticks when comparing their lengths and fit regions on top of each other to compare area
- use the everyday notion of 'how many fit' and count how many repeats of an object fit into or match another; e.g. How many pens fit along the table? How many potato prints cover the sheet? How many blocks fit in the box?
- count units and call it 'measuring'; e.g. *I measured and found the jar holds a bit more than 7 scoops.*
- use 'between' to describe measurements of uni-dimensional quantities (length, mass, capacity, time); e.g. *It weighs between 7 and 8 marbles.*
- refer informally to part-units when measuring uni-dimensional quantities; e.g. *Our room is 6 and a bit metres long.*

As s
Mat
to tl

- whi
  attri
  be i
  feat
  con
- may
  but
  not
  first
  leng
  me
  sto
- do
  ea
- m
  qu
  th
- ma
  uni
  di'
  th
- wh
  cen
  to '
  the
  an

Most students will enter the Matching and Comparing phase between 5 and 7 years of age.

As students move from the Emergent phase to the Matching and Comparing phase, they:

- may not 'conserve' measures; e.g. thinking that moving a rod changes its length, pouring changes 'how much', cutting up paper makes more surface

- may visually compare the size of two things, but make no effort to match; e.g. saying which stick is longer without lining up the bases or which sheet of paper is bigger without superimposing

- compare time spans but may not take into account different starting times; e.g. deciding that the TV program that finished latest was on longest

- use bipolar pairs but may have difficulty with some comparative terms; e.g. heft to decide which is heavier but say both are heavy because both hands go down

- may distinguish two attributes (such as tallness and weight) but not understand that the two attributes may lead to different orders of size for a collection, expecting the order for tallness and the order for weight to be the same

- while describing different attributes of the same thing (tall, thin and heavy) may be confused by a request to compare two things by different attributes, particularly if the comparisons lead to different orders

- often do not think to use counting to say how big or how much bigger; e.g. they may 'weigh' something by putting it into one side of a balance and smaller objects into the other side but not count the objects

During the Quantifying Phase

Students connect the two ideas of directly comparing the size of things and of deciding 'how many fit' and so come to an understanding that the count of actual or imagined repetitions of units gives an indication of size and enables two things to be compared without directly matching them.

As a result, they trust information about repetitions of units as an indicator of size and are prepared to use this in making comparisons of objects.

By the e... students

- attempt to representat... that the cu... doesn't cha... the same si...

- use the rep... carefully to possible, av... e.g. choose... the perime...

- know why... same size o... comparing

- see repeati... the unit ov... to filling or copies of it

- connect the... the numbe... calibrated s...

- make thing... uniform un... and metres

...t students will enter the ...ntifying phase between ...d 9 years of age.

...tudents move from the ...hing and Comparing phase ...e Quantifying phase, they:

...e knowing that ordering objects by different ...butes may lead to different orders, may still ...fluenced by the more dominant perceptual ...res; e.g. they may still think the tallest ...ainer holds the most

...count 'units' in order to compare two things ...be fairly casual in their repetition of units, ...noticing gaps or overlaps; e.g. placing the ...'unit' away from the end when measuring ...th, not worrying about spills when ...suring how much a container holds, not ...ping their claps immediately the music stops

...ot necessarily expect the same 'answer' ...time when deciding how many fit

...not think to use unit information to answer ...stions such as: Which cup holds more? Will ...table slide through the door?

...not see the significance of using a common ...to compare two things and, when using ...rent units, let the resulting number override ...r perceptual judgment

...e many will have learned to use the ...imetre marks on a conventional rule ...measure' lengths, often do not see ...connection between this process ...the repetition of units.

During the Measuring Phase

Students come to understand the unit as an amount (rather than an object or a mark on a scale) and to see the process of matching a unit with an object as equivalent to subdividing the object into bits of the same size as the unit and counting the bits.

As a result, they see that part-units can be combined to form whole units and they understand and trust the measurement as a property or description of the object being measured that does not change as a result of the choice or placement of units.

By the end of the Measuring phase, students typically:

- expect the same number of copies of the representation of their unit to match the object being measured regardless of how they arrange or place the copies

- understand that the smaller the unit the greater the number; e.g. are able to say which is the longer of a 1-kilometre walk and a 1400-metre walk.

- compose 'part-units' into wholes, understanding, for example, that a narrow garden bed may have an area of 5 or 6 square metres even though no whole 'metre squares' fit into the bed

- can themselves partition a rectangle into appropriate squares and use the array structure to work out how many squares are in the rectangle

- interpret the unnumbered graduations on a familiar whole-number scale

- understand the relationship between 'part-units' and the common metric prefixes; e.g. know that a unit can be broken into one hundred parts and each part will be a centi-unit

- work with provided measurement information alone; e.g. order measurements of capacity provided in different standard units, make things which meet measurement specifications.

M... en... be... ag...

As ... Me... Re...

- w... a... s... t... s...

- w... r... t... b... n... 2...

- w... u... j... s... s...

nd of the Quantifying phase, typically:

- ensure uniformity of
  ons of the unit; e.g. check
  is always full, the pencil
  nge length, the balls are
  re

- esentations of their unit
  make as close a match as
  oiding gaps and overlaps;
  a flexible tape to measure
  er of a curved shape

- hey need to choose the
  ojects to use as units when
  two quantities

- g one representation of
  r and over as equivalent
  matching with multiple

- repetition of a 'unit' with
  s on a whole-number
  cale

- to a specified length in
  s (including centimetres

- use provided measurements to make a decision about comparative size; e.g. use the fact that a friend's frog weighs 7 marbles to decide whether their own frog is heavier or lighter

- count units as a strategy to solve comparison problems such as: Whose frog is heavier? Put the jars in order from the one that holds the most to the one that holds the least.

- are prepared to say which is longer (heavier) based on information about the number of units matching each object

- think of different things having the same 'size'; e.g. use grid paper to draw different shapes with the same perimeter

- add measurements that they can readily think of in terms of repetitions of units; e.g. find the perimeter of a shape by measuring the sides and adding.

As students move from the Quantifying phase to the Measuring phase, they:

- while trying to make as close a match as possible to the thing to be measured, may find the desire to match closely overriding the need for consistency of unit; e.g. they may resort to 'filling' a region with a variety of different objects in order to cover it as closely as possible

- may not understand that the significance of having no gaps and overlaps is that the 'true' measurement is independent of the placement of the units

- may still think of the unit as an object and of measuring as 'fitting' in the social sense of the word (How many people fit in the elevator? How many beans in the jar?) and so have difficulty with the idea of combining part-units as is often needed in order to find the area of a region

- may confuse the unit (a quantity) with the instrument (or object) used to represent it; e.g. they may think a square metre has to be a square with sides of 1 metre, or that the markings on a ruler are the units

- may interpret whole numbered marks on a calibrated scale as units but may not interpret the meaning of unlabelled graduations.

st students will er the Relating phase ween 11 and 13 years of

students move from the asuring phase to the ating phase, they:

- hile partitioning a rectangle into
  propriate squares and using the array
  ucture to find its area, may not connect
  is with multiplying the lengths of the
  des of a rectangle to find its area

- hile understanding the inverse
  lationship between the unit and
  e number of units needed, may still
  e distracted by the numbers in
  easurements and ignore the units;
  g. say that 350 grams is more than
  kilograms

- hile converting between known standard
  nits, may treat related metric measures
  st as they would any other units, not
  eing the significance of the decimal
  ructure built into all metric measures.

During the Relating Phase

Students come to trust measurement information even when it is about things they cannot see or handle and to understand measurement relationships, both those between attributes and those between units.

As a result, they work with measurement information itself and can use measurements to compare things, including those they have not directly experienced, and to indirectly measure things.

By the end of the Relating phase, students typically:

- understand that known relationships between attributes can be used to find measurements that cannot be found directly; e.g. understand that we can use length measurements to work out area

- know that for figures of the same shape (that is, similar) the greater the length measures the greater the area measures, but this is not so if the figures are different shapes

- understand why the area of a rectangle and the volume of a rectangular prism can be found by multiplying its length dimensions and can use this for fractional side lengths

- think of the part-units themselves as units; e.g. a particular unit can be divided into one hundred parts and each part is then a centi-unit

- subdivide units to make measurements more accurate

- choose units that are sufficiently small (that is, accurate) to make the needed comparisons

- use their understanding of the multiplicative structure built into the metric system to move flexibly between related standard units; e.g. they interpret the 0.2 kilogram mark on a scale as 200 grams

- notice and reject unrealistic estimates and measurements, including of things they have not actually seen or experienced

- use relationships between measurements to find measures indirectly; e.g. knowing that 1 mL = 1 cm^3 they can find the volume of an irregular solid in cubic centimetres by finding how many millilitres of water it displaces using a capacity cylinder

Book 1

first steps ®

First Steps in
Mathematics
Measurement

- **Understand Units**
- **Direct Measure**

*Improving the mathematics
learning goals of students*

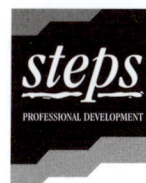

steps
PROFESSIONAL DEVELOPMENT

First Steps in Mathematics: Measurement
Understand Units, Direct Measure

Published in the United Kingdom by Steps Professional Development
Unit 78 Shrivenham 100 Business Park
Majors Road
Watchfield
Oxon
SN6 8TY

Steps Professional Development is a wholly owned subsidiary of Edith Cowan University in Perth, Western Australia. As a not-for-profit organisation, Steps Professional Development provides professional development and publishes resources for teachers in the areas of literacy (R-Y12), mathematics (R-Y9), and fundamental movement skills (R-Y3). Steps Professional development has offices in Australia, the United Kingdom, New Zealand and the United States.

© Department of Education and Training in Western Australia 2005

All rights reserved. No part of this book may be reproduced in any form or by any electronic or mechanical means, including information storage and retrieval systems, without the prior permission of the copyright owners. Apply in writing to the publishers.

Originally published in Australia by Rigby Heinemann, a division of Reed International Books Australia Pty Ltd.

ISBN 1-905232-27-6 FSiM Measurement Book 1

07 FSiM M Book 1   10 9 8 7 6 5 4 3 2 1

Reproduction and communication for educational purposes
The UK Copyright Act 1988(the Act) allows a maximum of one chapter or 10% of the pages of this book, whichever is the greater, to be reproduced and/ or communicated by any educational institution for its educational purposes provided that the educational institution (or the body that administers it) has given remuneration notices to Copyright Licensing Agency (CLA) under the Act.

For details of the CLA licence for educational institutions contact: www.CLA.co.uk

Reproduction and communication for other purposes
Except as permitted by the Act (for example, any fair dealing for the purposes of study, research, criticism or review) no part of this book may be reproduced, stored in a retrieval system, communicated or transmitted in any form or by any means without prior written permission. All enquiries should be made to the publisher at the address above. This book is not to be treated a s a blackline master; that is, any photocopying beyond fair dealing requires prior written permission.

Text by Sue Willis with Wendy Devlin, Lorraine Jacob, Beth Powell, Dianne Tomazos and Kaye Treacy.
Edited by Janet Mau
Text and cover design by Jennifer Johnston
Illustrations by Ian Forss,pp.1,2-3; all other illustrations by Neil Curtis

Printed by Craft Print International Limited

Contents

Introduction

The *First Steps in Mathematics* resource books and professional development are designed to help teachers plan, implement and evaluate the mathematics curriculum they provide for students. The series describes the key mathematical ideas students need to understand in order to achieve the principal learning goals of mathematics across the United Kingdom, Europe and around the world.

Unlike many resources that present mathematical concepts that have been logically ordered and prioritised by mathematicians or educators, *First Steps in Mathematics* follows a sequence derived from children's mathematical development. Each resource book is based on five years of research by a team of teachers from the Western Australian Department of Education and Training, and tertiary consultants led by Professor Sue Willis at Murdoch University.

The *First Steps in Mathematics* project team conducted an extensive review of international research literature, which revealed gaps in the field of knowledge about students' learning in mathematics. Many of these findings are detailed in the Background Notes that supplement the Key Understandings described in the *First Steps in Mathematics* resource books for Number.

Using tasks to replicate those in the research literature, team members interviewed hundreds of primary school children in diverse locations. Analysis of the data obtained from these interviews identified characteristic phases in the development of students' thinking about mathematical concepts.

The Diagnostic Maps – which appear in the resource books for Number, Measurement, Space, and Chance and data – describe these phases of development, exposing specific markers where students often lose, or never develop, the connection between mathematics and meaning. Thus, *First Steps in Mathematics* helps teachers systematically observe not only what mathematics individual children do, but how the children do the mathematics, and how to advance the children's learning.

It has never been more important to teach mathematics well. Globalisation and the increasing use of technology have created changing demands for the application of mathematics in all aspects of our lives. Teaching mathematics well to all students requires a high level of understanding of teaching and learning in mathematics and of mathematics itself. The *First Steps in Mathematics* series and professional development help teachers provide meaningful learning experiences and enhance their capacity to decide how best to help all students achieve the learning goals of mathematics.

CHAPTER 1

What Are the Features of this Resource Book?

The *First Steps in Mathematics: Measurement* Resource Books will help teachers to diagnose, plan, implement and judge the effectiveness of the teaching and learning experiences they provide for their students. *First Steps in Mathematics: Measurement* has two Resource Books. The first book examines the concepts relating to Understand Units and Direct Measure. The second book examines those relating to Indirect Measure and Estimate.

This Resource Book includes the following elements.

- Diagnostic Map
- Key Understandings
- Sample Learning Activities
- Sample Lessons
- 'Did You Know?' sections
- Background Notes

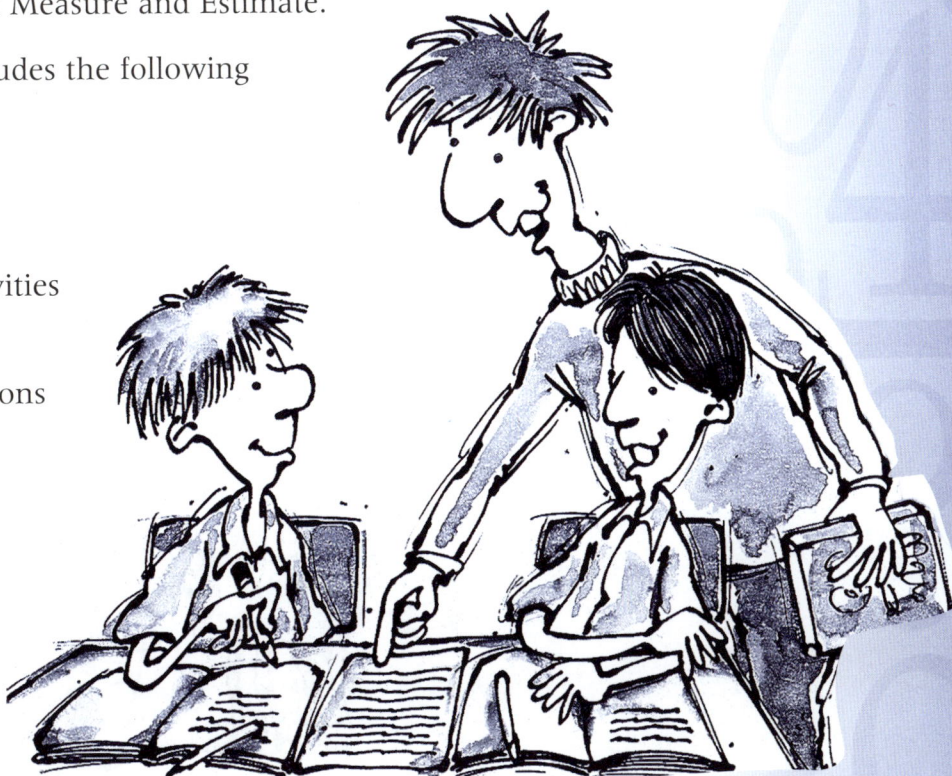

Diagnostic Maps

The purpose of the Diagnostic Maps is to help teachers:

- understand why students seem to be able to do some things and not others
- realise why some students may be experiencing difficulty while others are not
- indicate the challenges students need to move their thinking forward, to refine their preconceptions, overcome any misconceptions, and so achieve the learning goals
- interpret their students' responses to activities.

Each map includes key indicators and consequences of students' understanding and growth. This information is crucial for teachers making judgments about their students' level of understanding of mathematics. It enhances teachers' judgments about what to teach, to whom and when to teach it.

Using the Diagnostic Maps

The Diagnostic Maps are intended to assist teachers as they plan their mathematics curriculum. The Diagnostic Maps describe the characteristic phases in the development of students' thinking about the major concepts in each set of learning goals. The descriptions of the phases help teachers make judgments about students' understandings of the mathematical concepts.

The text in the shaded sections of each map describes students' major preoccupations, or focus, *during* that phase of thinking about the mathematics strand.

The 'By the end' section of each phase provides examples of what students typically think and are able to do as a result of having worked through the phase.

The achievements in the 'By the end' section should be read in conjunction with the 'As students move from' section. The 'As students move from' section includes the preconceptions, partial conceptions and misconceptions that students may have developed along the way. These provide the learning challenges for the next phase.

Together, the 'By the end' and 'As students move from' sections illustrate that while students might have developed a range of important understandings as they passed through the phase, they might also have developed some unconventional or unhelpful ideas at the same time. Both of these sections of the Diagnostic Map are intended as a useful guide only.

Key Understandings

The Key Understandings are the cornerstone of the *First Steps in Mathematics* series. The Key Understandings:

- describe the mathematical ideas, or concepts, which students need to know

- suggest what experiences teachers should plan for

- provide a basis for the recognition and assessment of what students already know and still need to know in order to progress
- indicate the emphasis of the curriculum at particular stages
- provide content and pedagogic advice to assist with planning the curriculum at the classroom and whole-school levels.

Sample Learning Activities

For each Key Understanding, there are Sample Learning Activities that teachers could use to develop the mathematical ideas of the Key Understanding. The activities are organised into three broad groups.

- Beginning activities are suitable for Kindergarten/Reception to Year 3 students.
- Middle activities cater for Year 3 to Year 5 students.
- Later activities are designed for Year 5 to Year 7 students.

If students in the later years have not had enough prior experience, then teachers may need to select and adapt activities from earlier groups.

Sample Lessons

The Sample Lessons illustrate some of the ways teachers can use the sample Learning Activities for the Beginning, Middle and Later groups. The emphasis is on how teachers can focus students' attention on the mathematics during the learning activity.

'Did You Know?' Sections

For some of the Key Understandings, there are 'Did You Know?' sections. These sections highlight common understandings and misunderstandings that students have. Some 'Did You Know?' sections also suggest diagnostic activities that teachers may wish to try with their students.

Background Notes

The Background Notes supplement the information provided in the Key Understandings. These notes are designed to help teachers develop a more in-depth knowledge of what is required as students achieve the mathematics learning goals.

The Background Notes are based on extensive research and are more detailed than the descriptions of the mathematical ideas in the Key Understandings. The content of the Background Notes varies. Sometimes, they describe how students learn specific mathematical ideas. Other notes explain the mathematics that may be new or unfamiliar to teachers.

CHAPTER 2

Understand Units

> **Decide what needs to be measured by selecting what attributes to measure and what units to use.**

This chapter will support teachers in developing teaching and learning plans that relate to this outcome:

Overall Description

Students know that the same things can be compared and ordered by different attributes, such as length, capacity or mass, depending on the purpose of the measurement. They understand that choosing a different attribute will make a difference to the order. They use appropriate comparative language to describe their comparisons, such as taller/shorter, wider/narrower.

Students understand that we use a unit when we want to quantify 'how big' or 'how much bigger' and that generally measurements are only as accurate as the unit they choose. When deciding what attribute to measure and how accurate they need to be (that is, what unit to use), they consider both the purpose of the measurement and the closeness of the comparisons to be made. They know, for example, that hand spans are probably good enough units to use to check whether a cupboard will fit a corner, but if it looks like being a tight squeeze, a smaller unit should be chosen.

Students understand that standard units are not more accurate than non-standard units, but that using standard units can help them in record-keeping and communication and are usually necessary when using formulae.

Students use common measuring equipment and graduated scales, such as rulers, clocks and kitchen scales. They choose equipment or techniques to suit their situation. They express measurements in correct units and use their understanding of the common metric prefixes to move flexibly between units and to judge size.

Key Understandings

Teachers need to plan learning experiences that include and develop the following Key Understandings (KU). The learning experiences should connect to students' current knowledge and understandings rather than to their year level.

Key Understanding	Stage of Primary Schooling— Major Emphasis	KU Description	Sample Learning Activities
KU1 We can compare things by how much of a particular attribute each has. Different attributes may result in different orders.	Beginning ✔✔✔ Middle ✔✔ Later ✔✔	page 8	Beginning, page 10 Middle, page 12 Later, page 14
KU2 There are special words and phrases that help us to describe and compare quantity.	Beginning ✔✔ Middle ✔✔ Later ✔✔	page 16	Beginning, page 18 Middle, page 20 Later, page 22
KU3 To measure something means to say how much of a particular attribute it has. We measure by choosing a unit and working out how many of the unit it takes to match the thing.	Beginning ✔✔✔ Middle ✔✔✔ Later ✔✔	page 24	Beginning, page 26 Middle, page 28 Later, page 30
KU4 The instrument we choose to represent our unit should relate well to the attribute to be measured and be easy to repeat to match the thing to be measured.	Beginning ✔✔ Middle ✔✔✔ Later ✔✔	page 38	Beginning, page 40 Middle, page 42 Later, page 44
KU5 Measurements of continuous quantities are always approximate. Measurements can be made more accurate by choosing smaller units, subdividing units and other strategies.	Beginning ✔ Middle ✔✔✔ Later ✔✔✔	page 46	Beginning, page 48 Middle, page 50 Later, page 52
KU6 Our choice of attribute and unit depends upon what we are trying to measure and why.	Beginning ✔ Middle ✔✔ Later ✔✔✔	page 54	Beginning, page 56 Middle, page 58 Later, page 60
KU7 Standard units help us to interpret, communicate and calculate measurements.	Beginning ✔ Middle ✔✔ Later ✔✔✔	page 66	Beginning, page 68 Middle, page 70 Later, page 72
KU8 The relationships between standard units in the metric system help us to judge size, move between units and do calculations.	Beginning ✔ Middle ✔✔ Later ✔✔✔	page 74	Beginning, page 76 Middle, page 78 Later, page 80

Key

✔✔✔ The development of this Key Understanding is a major focus of planned activities.

✔✔ The development of this Key Understanding is an important focus of planned activities.

✔ Some activities may be planned to introduce this Key Understanding, to consolidate it, or to extend its application. The idea may also arise incidentally in conversations and routines that occur in the classroom.

KEY UNDERSTANDING 1

We can compare things by how much of a particular attribute each has. Different attributes may result in different orders.

Comparison by quantity underlies many of our descriptions of the world. Sometimes we are explicit, for example, we say, *It takes longer by bus than by train*. At other times, the comparison remains implicit, for example, we say, *He is tall*, but mean *He is tall compared to other boys* or *He is tall compared to me*. We also say, *She is 1.40 metres tall* and mean that she is 1.4 times as big as a standard unit called a metre.

Key Understanding 1 relates to the development of students' capacity to differentiate types of bigness and smallness. Most students notice different attributes from an early age: *That drink is too much for me, I need to speak louder so they'll hear, I'm too big to fit*. Their early descriptions of objects, however, are likely to refer to a general perception of 'bigness' or 'smallness'. Students need to develop the understanding that we can compare things by how much they have of a *particular* attribute and we can then put them in order, from less to *more of that attribute*. We might, for example, compare suitcases by capacity (how much clothing they will hold). We might also compare them by mass (how heavy they will be to carry when empty). Television programs can be compared by finishing time (which television program finishes earliest) or elapsed time (which program is shortest).

Objects have many attributes, but only some of these attributes are readily described in terms of 'more' or 'less' and used to put things in order. Although we can compare the attributes of colour, taste, shape or texture, for example, we do not usually think of them in terms of 'more' and 'less' and 'how much' and so we do not usually order by these attributes or think of them as mathematical attributes. (Of course, we do refer to the strength of colour or taste and can order by concentration rates.) During the primary years, students should develop the capacity to focus upon and distinguish between the attributes commonly used to order objects and events: length, area, volume or capacity, mass, angle and time. In doing so, they should come to understand that:

- for certain attributes, the idea of having 'less' or 'more' of the attribute makes common sense

- we can use these attributes to compare and order objects or events

- the order of the objects or events may change if we focus on a different attribute.

Students who are through the Emergent Phase are aware of length, mass, capacity and time as attributes of objects and events and can use them to put two or three obviously different things in order.

Students who are through the Matching and Comparing Phase understand that comparing by one attribute may produce a different order to comparing by another. They are able to focus upon a particular attribute in practical familiar situations. They may have found, for example, that sometimes the tallest jar holds the most and sometimes it does not. As a result, they may conclude that if we want the most to drink we need to focus upon the capacity of the jar, not its height.

Students who are through the Quantifying Phase have a more generalised understanding that different attributes may lead to different orders, although they are likely to be tricked by complex situations. They may, for example, incorrectly assume that if the distance around one rectangle is bigger so, too, must be the area.

Students who are through the Measuring Phase consistently distinguish the time it is now from how much time something has taken. They distinguish perimeter from area and know that the figure with the biggest area need not have the biggest perimeter and vice versa.

SAMPLE LEARNING ACTIVITIES

Beginning ✔✔✔

Storing or Selecting Materials

Invite students to compare and order by attribute when storing or selecting equipment. For example, before packing away boxes (glue bottles) used for another activity, ask students to think of how to sort them and pack them in order, from the largest to the smallest. Focus on height, width or length at separate times. Or, ask students to find a skipping rope of suitable length (ball of suitable size) for an activity.

Hefting Objects

Invite students to heft objects ranging from large and light to small and heavy (e.g. cushions, balls, fruit, sponges, marbles, rocks, fruit). Ask: Is yours heavier than this small one? Which ones will we leave for an adult to lift?

Jellies

Organise students into groups and have them order jelly moulds by different attributes; for example, from tall to short, fat to thin, needing the largest plate to sit on to needing the smallest, from most jelly to the least amount of jelly. Ask: Which one has the most jelly? Why does this jelly need a bigger plate than the tallest jelly? Adapt this to sand castles by having students build sand castles using the lids as the base. Ask: Which is the biggest? Is this one on the big lid bigger than this tall one? Which sand castle has the most sand?

Play Dough

Extend 'Jellies' by having groups of students use play dough to make snakes ranging from short and fat through to long and thin. Invite them to order them by length. When they have done this, ask: How can you tell which one is longest? Draw out from students the need for the snakes to be lined up against a baseline, such as the edge of the desk, so that their lengths can be compared. Then, ask students to coil the snakes and reorder them by the table space they will take up. Ask students to reform the play dough, roll it out and use lids to cut scones. Ask them to order the scones by area, make piles of same-area scones, and order the piles by height. Have students reform the play dough again. Invite them to roll it into balls and order them by height, by looking from the edge of the table, and mass, using balance scales.

Length

Provide lengths of string (wool, rope, paper tape, straws, matches, chopsticks, popsticks) for students to choose from and use in play, construction and collage activities. Ask: How long? Which length will be high enough (long enough) to go around (to go along, to reach the other side, to go far enough down)?

Hairy Maclary

Read some Hairy Maclary stories to the class (Lynley Dodd, Viking Kestrel Picture Books). Ask students to explain how the dogs vary in size in different ways. Ask: Which dog is big? How is it bigger than Hairy Maclary? Which dog could you lift up? Which dog will be heavier than Hairy Maclary? Which dog fits through the hole in the hedge? Follow the same process with other stories. (See Key Understanding 2.)

Area

Invite students to select and cover regions (e.g. choose a rug to cover a toy, spread paste using a knife, squeegee or brush, help cover a table top with paper to design a model of a town). Ask: Will it cover the surface? Are there any gaps? Did it go over the edge? Encourage students to explain to others what they have to consider to cover a region in the same way.

Hefting Closed Tubs

Store construction and collage materials (e.g. matchsticks, washers, popsticks) in identical closed tubs. Invite students to heft each tub and say what they think each tub is holding because of its weight. Open tubs for students to talk about the contents and why one tub was heavier than another. Ask: Why is the matchstick tub lighter than the washer tub? Add an empty closed tub and invite students to heft it. Ask: What do you think is inside this tub? Is this tub the lightest? As students view and handle containers, ask: How could we order the containers on a shelf from heaviest to lightest? What other ways could the containers be ordered?

Pour to Decide

Ask students to place cups in order of those that hold the most to those that hold the least. Invite them to check by filling the cup they think holds more and pouring the amount into the second cup and so on. Encourage them to talk about why the order was right or wrong (e.g. *I thought the tall one was biggest, but that fat one holds more*). Repeat with the same cups over a few days to enable students to compare the capacity of the cups in their mind's eye. (See Key Understanding 2; link to Direct Measure, Key Understanding 1.)

SAMPLE LEARNING ACTIVITIES

Middle ✔✔

Stretching

Have students compare and order materials (e.g. string, wool, elastic, jelly snake, liquorice) by how much each will stretch. Ask: Which attribute (length, area, volume) is being used to order them? (Link to Direct Measure, Key Understanding 1.)

Changing Attributes of a Balloon

Organise students into groups and give each group a selection of different-shaped balloons. Have one student blow up a balloon. Ask: Which attributes of the balloon have changed? (length, area, volume). Invite students to blow up the rest of their balloons and order them by something they can measure. Ask: How would this order change if we used distance around the balloon instead of volume? (Link to Direct Measure, Key Understandings 1 and 2.)

Judging the Biggest

Invite students to identify the attributes that could be compared to judge which is the biggest pumpkin (apple, potato). For example, the largest pumpkin (apple, potato) could be the one with the longest circumference or distance around (length), the one that is the heaviest (mass), the one that would give the most to eat (volume or mass of flesh), the one with the largest amount of skin (surface area), the one that is tallest (length). Through discussion, arrive at attributes that are reasonable for the largest pumpkin (apple, potato). Ask students to use the attributes to order them from smallest to largest. (Link to Direct Measure, Key Understandings 1 and 2.)

Organising Drink Containers

Discuss with students how drink containers may be organised in a supermarket. Invite small groups of students to try different arrangements based on attributes such as height, capacity, mass, brand, type of drink, colour. Ask: Which arrangements focus on quantities (how much) and which focus on other things? Why is mass not important for stacking? (because stability and not wasting space are more important)
(See Key Understanding 2.)

Time Taken Getting to School

Have students order the time taken for various activities compared to ordering by other attributes. For example, invite them to work out how long it usually takes to get to school. Ask: Who takes the longest to get to school? How does that student get to school? (e.g. by car, by bus, riding a bicycle, walking). How far away does that person live? Does the student who lives closest to the school take the least time to get there? What else do you need to take into account?

Comparing Polygons

Organise students into pairs and give each pair a pattern block hexagon, square and triangle. Ask students to order them by area. When they have done this, ask them to compare angles by superimposing one shape on top of another to see which angle is larger. Have them order the shapes by the size of the angles. Ask: How else could you order them? (Link to Direct Measure, Key Understanding 1, and Indirect Measure, Key Understanding 1.)

Start and Finish Times

Give groups of students information about the start and finish times of nearby schools and the start and finish times of their recess and lunch breaks. Ask them to order the schools by which start first, which finish first and which have the longest lunch and recess time. Ask: Do the schools that start early finish early? Do the schools that have short lunch and recess time finish early? How did you work out the order of the start times? How did you work out the order of the amount of time taken for lunch and recess? How was working out the order of the start times different to working out how much time was taken? (Link to Indirect Measure, Key Understanding 4.)

Mass or Volume

Present students with a collection of items from the supermarket and ask them to classify them according to whether they use mass or volume measures. Ask: Why is ice cream and milk sold in litres? How are these two items the same? Why is rice sold by mass, not volume?

Twelve Tiles

Ask students to use 12 tiles to construct as many different rectangles as possible and record each one on grid paper. Have students order the shapes by the distance around each one. Ask: Can you order the shapes by their area? Why? Why not?

Perimeter and Area

Organise students into pairs and give each pair a geoboard and a piece of string. Have them tie a knot in the piece of string at 24 centimetres and use it to construct a shape with a perimeter of 24 centimetres. Invite students to make other shapes with the same perimeter. Have them record each shape on grid paper. Ask: How does the size of the area change?

SAMPLE LEARNING ACTIVITIES

Later ✔✔

Comparing Two People

Organise students into pairs and invite them to think of what measurements they could take to compare one another. Ask them to take the measurements and write comparisons of themselves; for example, *I am 4 centimetres taller than my partner, but my arm span is 3 centimetres shorter and I weigh 1 kilogram less*. Invite students to classify their measures into length, mass, volume and area. Ask: Which attributes were measured the most? Which attributes were not measured? What would you have to do to measure these attributes? (Link to Key Understanding 3.)

Ordering Animals

Invite pairs of students to choose ten animals and decide what they could measure to order the animals. Ask: Can you order according to colour (habitat, diet)? Why? Why not? Ask students to specify what measurement they will take for each attribute. Ask: What length are you measuring? Have students order the animals according to each attribute they have measured. Ask: Are the animals in the same order for each attribute? Why? Why not?

Sweets

Provide packets of sweets that are wrapped individually to groups of students. Say: Whoever thought of making this sweet would have had to think of a lot of different things when they were designing it. Ask: What attributes would that person have had to think about? Draw out the range of possibilities related to mass, volume and length, such as the weight of the sweet, the dimensions of the sweet, the wrapping paper, the print on the wrapping paper and the various attributes involved in packaging the sweets in boxes or bags. Invite students to invent a new kind of sweet and write up its specifications with all the measurements they have discussed. (Link to Key Understanding 6.)

Identikit

Display about 15 objects at the front of the class. Organise students into pairs and ask each pair to choose one of the objects and write a measurement identikit for it using attributes of length, area, mass and volume or capacity. Return all the objects to the front of the class, collect the identikits and invite each pair to choose a different identikit to solve by matching the descriptions to an object. Encourage them to justify their selections; for example, *I measured the surface area of the cube and found it was 54 square centimetres*. (See Key Understanding 2; link to Key Understanding 6.)

Baby Measurements

Ask students to bring in their baby measurements. Invite them to take the same measurements now and compare them. Ask: Which attributes have increased the most? Which have increased the least? Why? (Link to Key Understanding 6 and Sample Lesson 3, page 63.)

Doctor Measurements

Ask students who have been to the doctor recently to describe what measurements the doctors took. Discuss the attributes that are being measured each time and what they mean. For example, ask: What are doctors measuring when they measure lung capacity? What capacity are they talking about? What other things can have their capacity measured? What are doctors measuring when they measure blood pressure? What other things involve measuring pressure? What measurements involve time? (Link to Direct Measure, Key Understanding 6.)

Different Orders

Have students explain why the same things may have been ordered in different ways. For example, say: Here is a problem some students were asked to work out. Their school had two pieces of land, one a rectangle and one a triangle. The school wanted to choose the largest one for a garden bed. Joshua thought the rectangular garden was bigger than the triangular bed, but Su-Lin thought the triangle shape was bigger. Ask: Why did the students think different things? What could Joshua be using to help him make his decision? How could you tell for sure which piece of land was bigger? Then, say: Another group of students were asked to put four full lunch boxes in order of size. They all came up with different answers. Ask: How could the same objects have been put into different orders? (some could have measured the capacity, some the surface area, some the height) (See Sample Lesson 2, page 35, and Key Understanding 3.)

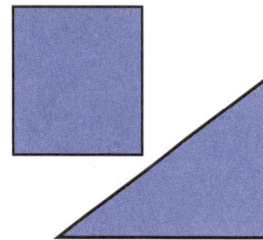

Swimming Pools

Have students draw different shapes that have the same area. Say: A swimming pool company charges the same price to build any swimming pool, no matter what shape, so long as it has a water surface area of 18 square metres. Invite students to design different-shaped pools and demonstrate that the pools all have a surface area of 18 square metres.

Pool Perimeters

Ask students to work out the perimeter of each pool designed in 'Swimming Pools'. Ask: Which pool needs the longest length of tiling around the edge? Which needs the shortest? If you owned the pool company and were paying for the line of tiles around the pool, which shaped pool (with an area of 18 square metres) would be the cheapest to build?

KEY UNDERSTANDING 2

There are special words and phrases that help us to describe and compare quantity.

From a very early age, students will have ideas about 'more', 'less' and 'equal amounts' and will have some of the language of comparison. Their language should develop and be refined throughout the primary years so that they are able to use general comparative language (big, small, more, less), different words associated with one attribute (tall, short, wide, narrow, long, length, distance) and comparative language associated with particular attributes (tall, taller, tallest, as tall as).

Students are likely to understand some 'comparative pairs' before others (e.g. multi-dimensional pairs such as big/small before uni-dimensional pairs such as high/low) and 'positive' members of pairs before 'negative' members (e.g. tall before short, heavy before light). Comparative pairs need explicit attention. Also, the subtleties of comparative terms are to an extent culture specific. For example, Europeans determine a 'bigger' fish by its length, but the people of north-east Arnhem Land compare the size of fish by their girth. Assuming we speak a common language is often to the mathematical disadvantage of students for whom English is a second language. Equally, however, avoiding the use of standard comparative language will disadvantage students in the longer term. All students should experience the use of the language of quantity and comparison in a wide range of contexts and the subtleties and cultural differences in the use of terms such as 'wide' and 'narrow' should be addressed throughout all of the primary years.

Students also need to learn to use the terms length, area, volume, capacity and mass appropriately as they engage in activities in Direct Measurement and Indirect Measurement. They might, for example, initially talk about 'distance around' and 'amount of fence needed' for a paddock as well as 'how much grass' is inside the fence. In order to develop this Key Understanding, the language of length and area should be modelled by the teacher and situations structured so that the students themselves have plenty of opportunity to 'try out' their use of terms such as length, width, perimeter and area in sensible contexts.

Students who are through the Emergent Phase respond appropriately to and use for themselves everyday comparative language associated with length, mass and capacity, using the language forms of their own communities. As they progress through the next several levels, their use of standard terms should develop.

Students who are through the Matching and Comparing Phase distinguish length from area in situations where the context helps them make sense of the terms. They also associate the word mass with 'heaviness' and 'capacity' with how much something holds.

Students who are through the Quantifying Phase respond appropriately to and use the everyday language of attributes and comparison in conventional ways. They also will respond appropriately to the term 'perimeter' in situations where the contexts assist their interpretation, students who are through the Measuring Phase have a clear understanding of the distinction between perimeter and area and area and volume.

? *Did You Know?*

Many students confuse 'the time' with 'how much time'. A teacher of 7-year-olds asked them to draw pictures of themselves going to bed and getting up and to write their names and the times underneath. They then sorted their pictures into groups by time. Asked to work out who was in bed the longest, most responded that it was those who went to bed at 7 p.m. In vain, the teacher pointed out that one child who went to bed at 7 p.m. was up at 6 a.m., while another who went to bed at 7:30 p.m. wasn't up until 7:30 a.m. The students were convinced that those who went to bed first were in bed longest.

The teacher thought that probably the students could not work out how much time they were in bed, so she helped them to mark a long strip with hours of the day a centimetre apart. They then coloured the strip between when they went to bed and when they woke and cut off the uncoloured parts. The teacher then made a column graph by using the paper strips and lining up the bases. She suggested that the graph would help the students to find out who was in bed longest. To her surprise, the students rejected her approach, *You've made a mistake — you've made us all go to bed at the same time.*

The students have not yet understood the difference between time and elapsed time.

SAMPLE LEARNING ACTIVITIES

Beginning ✔✔

Describing and Comparing Quantity

Give students instructions and ask them questions involving language that describes and compares quantities. For example, ask: Did you use the heaviest or lightest truck today? How do you know your line is longer than your partner's? Or, say: Turn the paper so that it is wider than it is high. Make a narrower gap between the lines.

Hairy Maclary

Extend the Beginning Sample Learning Activity 'Hairy Maclary' (Key Understanding 1) by asking: Which dog is the smallest? Do you think you could lift Hercules Morse? Why? Why not? Why didn't Muffin MacLay fit through the hole in the hedge? Encourage students to name different lengths; for example, 'tall, thin legs', 'wide, thick neck', 'long, thin tail', 'short, wide snout', 'narrow ears'. Ask: Which dog is wider (lower, shorter, faster, slower, could fit through this space)?

More Stories

Extend 'Hairy Maclary' to other literature for students to notice and use terms to describe the different attributes of the 'props' and characters.

Full and Empty

Have students use various containers to pour from one to another during play and food preparation. Focus students on 'full', 'overflowing', 'empty', 'not very full', 'some left over' and 'needs more'.

Pour to Decide

Extend the Beginning Sample Learning Activity 'Pour to Decide' (Key Understanding 1). As students pour from one container to another to compare capacity, focus them on describing how much a container will hold (e.g. holds more, holds less, holds a lot, doesn't hold very much, left over, more than, less than, level, heaped). (See also Direct Measure, Key Understanding 1.)

Sorting

Invite students to sort objects (e.g. shells, leaves, rocks) into groups and then order them by size. Ask: Which part of the shell (leaf, rock) did you look at to judge the size? Have them describe, draw and label how they grouped and ordered the shells (leaves, rocks).

KU 2

Short and Tall Posters

Invite students to make posters to show 'what is short to a giraffe', and 'what is tall to a mouse'. Ask: Does anything appear in both posters? How can the dog be both short and tall?

Colloquial Terms

Model the correct word when students use colloquial terms to describe order. For example, when describing by height, they may say, *This one's really tall, this one's a big bit tall, this is a little bit tall and this one's a bit tall*. Respond by affirming their ordering and say, for example: Yes, that one is the tallest, that one is tall and that one is shorter and that one's the shortest of all.

What Am I?

Invite students to play 'What Am I?' using measurement language. For example, say: I am heavier than a pencil, but lighter than a glue stick (wider than a sharpener but narrower than a bucket, hold more than a teaspoon but less than a drink bottle). What am I? Encourage students to ask questions to help their thinking (e.g. *Are you narrower than ... ?*)

SAMPLE LEARNING ACTIVITIES

Middle ✔✔

Bigger Foot

Tell students you heard someone say, 'I've got a bigger foot than you.' Ask: What measurements do you think they were thinking of? Organise students into pairs and invite them to make a cut-out shape of their foot. Encourage them to talk about the length, width, perimeter and area of their foot in comparison to their partner's foot. For example, ask: Is your foot longer than Ahmed's? Is it wider? Is it further around? Does it take up more space? (Link to Key Understanding 1.)

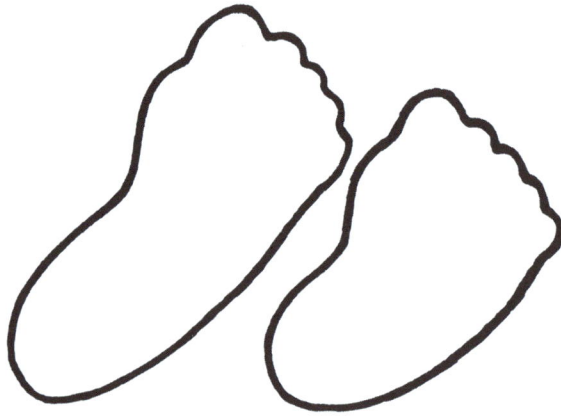

Comparative Words

Brainstorm and list pairs of comparative words that describe more and less length, area, volume and capacity, time and mass. Invite students to illustrate a chosen pair. Display the illustrations with the words.

General or Special Words

After activities such as 'Comparative Words', categorise the words according to whether they are 'general' or 'special' words. For example, 'bigger' can refer to lots of different things about lots of different objects, but 'taller' is a special word referring to height or how high from the ground. Anything can be 'bigger', but only some sorts of things would be 'taller'.

'What Am I?' Riddles

Invite students to write 'What Am I?' riddles using the pairs of words from the class list of words developed in 'Comparative Words'. For example, *I am shorter than a ruler, but longer than a pencil sharpener. I am heavier than a sweet but lighter than a book. What am I?* (Link to Estimate, Key Understanding 1.)

Organising Drink Containers

Extend the Middle Sample Learning Activity 'Organising Drink Containers' (Key Understanding 1) by having students order the collection of drink containers and then write a label for each item in the order. For example, when stacked by height, encourage them to use the labels 'short', 'tall', 'tallest'. When stacked by mass, encourage them to use the labels 'light', 'heavy', 'heaviest'. When stacked by capacity, encourage them to use the labels 'holds a bit', 'holds a lot', 'holds the most'. Ask: What does the word 'mass' describe? What does the word 'capacity' describe?

Science Activities

During science activities involving change (e.g. monitoring the growth of plants, animals, crystals), encourage students to select words to describe how each attribute has changed (e.g. longer, greater area, wider). Have students use these words in the written reports of the experiments. For example, when students are considering length, they might write: *The plant became taller and each of its leaves became wider.*

Wrapping Presents

Invite students to use newspaper to work out how much material they need to buy to wrap presents for Mothers' Day. Organise them into pairs and give each pair a shape or box to act as a present. While the students are working, ask: Do you need to know the length measurements or area measurements? How does the volume of the present affect how much wrapping paper you need? How does the surface area affect how much wrapping paper you need? Have students write definitions in their own words for each of the attributes of length, area, volume and surface area. (Link to Estimate, Key Understanding 1.)

Twelve Tiles

Extend the Middle Sample Learning Activity 'Twelve Tiles' (Key Understanding 1). During the activity, ask students to use the word 'perimeter' to describe the distance around the different shapes.

SAMPLE LEARNING ACTIVITIES

Later ✔✔

Identikit

Have students use attribute language and the language of the standard units to describe objects. For example, extend the Later Sample Learning Activity 'Identikit' (Key Understanding 1) by asking students to refer to at least two attributes. For example: *My object has an area of 600 square centimetres, but its volume is much less than 600 cubic centimetres.* After the activity, encourage students to reflect on how they arrived at their clues. For example: *Mine was a page. About six MAB flats fit on a page, so its area is about 600 square centimetres. Its volume is much less than 600 cubic centimetres because a page is lots thinner than a flat.* (Link to Key Understanding 1, Estimate, Key Understanding 3, and Indirect Measure, Key Understanding 1.)

Sweets Container

Encourage students to use terms associated with the attributes of area, volume or capacity in order to make comparisons and discuss relationships between measures. For example, ask students to design and make the largest possible cylindrical-shaped closed sweet container using a single sheet of A4 paper. Have them use beans or something similar to test the capacity of their container. Invite them to compare and discuss the relative dimensions of their containers and the resulting capacities. For example, *My cylinder is shorter than yours but it has a greater capacity. A smaller circumference doesn't always mean less capacity.* (Link to Direct Measure, Key Understandings 3 and 5, and Indirect Measure, Key Understanding 2.)

Big Fish

Encourage students to collect descriptions of situations in which people use 'bigness' to describe relative size or quantity and examine the possible confusion of interpretations that could occur. For example, say: When people in north-east Arnhem Land talk about a 'big' fish, they use their hands to represent the 'width' of the fish, whereas European Australians would use their hands to show the 'length'. Ask: Can you think of any times when you misunderstood someone because you misunderstood what they meant by a particular size word? (Link to Key Understanding 1.)

Different Types of Length

Have students brainstorm the different types of lengths that can be measured (e.g. height, circumference, depth, width, tallness, thickness). Organise students into groups and assign a type of length to each group. Ask them to list all the objects and situations they can think of that have that type of length (e.g. thickness: piece of paper, trunk of a tree, sheet of steel). Invite groups to compare lists and identify objects and situations that occur in more than one list. Encourage students to clarify what kind of length they mean for these common situations. Ask: Do 'thickness' and 'width' mean the same thing when referring to the trunk of a tree? What about a sheet of paper? (Link to Key Understanding 1.)

> ## KEY UNDERSTANDING 3
>
> *To measure something means to say how much of a particular attribute it has. We measure by choosing a unit and working out how many of the unit it takes to match the thing.*

We can directly and indirectly compare the size of things and put them in order without using numbers. When we want to describe 'how big' something is or 'how much bigger' one thing is than another, however, we use numbers. The process of quantifying attributes is usually called measuring.

To directly measure 'how heavy' a rock is, we might choose the mass of a marble as our unit of mass, count how many marbles it takes to balance the rock (as well as we can) and conclude that the rock is 11 marbles heavy. We might choose the time of one full swing of a locket as our unit of time and use it to measure how much time it took to walk across a room, concluding that, 'I took seven full swings, Sam took nine. He took two full swings longer.' In fact, we don't always have to actually match an object or event with a unit because we have also developed a range of indirect measurement techniques (see Indirect Measure), but the underlying idea is always to quantify an attribute by finding out 'how many' of the units match or fit the object or event.

Students need to internalise the following ideas if they are to fully understand how 'measuring' works.

- We can use numbers to describe the size of a thing by selecting a unit and counting how many repeats of the unit it takes to match the thing as closely as possible.

- A unit is itself a quantity; that is, it is the mass of the marble that is the unit, not the marble itself.

- The size of something doesn't change when you use a different-sized unit to measure it, but the number of units taken to match it may change.

- We can say which of two things is bigger by comparing how many of the same unit match each.

These ideas develop more slowly than is often recognised. Having developed these ideas, however, students can see *why*:

- we should generally use the same unit repeatedly to measure an object
- when comparing two things, the same unit should be chosen for each.

Students who are through the Matching and Comparing Phase of the outcome will correctly respond to a request to, for example, 'count how many pens fit across the table' and may have learned to call this 'measuring'. For them, however, the task is one of counting to see 'how many fit' in much the same way as we might ask how many people fit in the car or how many times did you turn before the music finished. Even prompted, they do not use this information as a measurement to answer questions such as, 'Will the table slide through the door?'

As students move into the Quantifying Phase they will use a unit to decide which of two things is bigger, when prompted, but may be 'tricked' by conflicting information. For example, they may believe that the size can change when a different unit is used.

For students who are through the Quantifying Phase, the ideas they have developed about comparing by attributes and 'how many units fit' have come together and they understand what it means to measure. Unprompted, they will use a measurement to decide whether one thing is bigger or smaller than another, understand why it helps to use the same size unit repeatedly to measure a thing and why it is necessary to use same unit for each quantity when comparisons are to be made.

Students in the Measuring Phase understand the unit as a quantity and so, for example, realise that a square of side one metre can be cut and rearranged and still be the same unit, that is, 'a square metre'.

KU 3

SAMPLE LEARNING ACTIVITIES

Beginning ✔✔✔

Trains

Ask students to make trains from blocks. Invite them to count how many carriages long their train is. Ask: Is your train longer than Tracey's? She has six carriages. How many blocks long is that train? Is your train longer or shorter? How did you work that out? (See Direct Measure, Key Understandings 2 and 3.)

Using a Balance Scale

After students have hefted two objects, ask them to place the first object they hefted in one side of a balance scale. Invite them to place units (e.g. marbles, washers) in the other side one at a time and count how many units match the weight of their object to make the scales balance. Encourage them to describe how heavy their object is. (e.g. *My bottle weighs the same as 28 marbles*.) (See Sample Lesson 1 in Direct Measure, page 99.)

Balancing Tools

Extend 'Using a Balance Scale' by making other balancing tools (e.g. see-saws, buckets on ropes, rulers on cotton reels). Focus on matching weight and balancing by asking: How many marbles (washers) does it take to balance this doll (truck)?

Different Units

As students use balancing equipment in play or activities, have them use and record how many different units match the weight of their object. Ask: How can your object be the same as 12 washers and the same as only 8 marbles?

Desk Through the Doorway

Present students with length problem situations where measuring rather than directly comparing is required. For example, ask: Will that heavy desk over there slide through this doorway? How do you know? Prompt with questions. Ask: How wide is the desk? How wide is the doorway? How many pens fit across the desk? How many pens fit across the doorway? Does the pen measure help you decide?

Fish Container

Give groups of students some large containers and ask them to choose an object (e.g. cup, jug) to use as a unit to find the container with the largest volume to keep a fish in. Ask: How can you use this object to find out the size of your containers? What is the size of your unit? What is the size of the largest container? How do you know it is the largest?

Beads on a String

Invite students to select one length of string from a range of three lengths and one bead size from a range of sizes to make a necklace. When they have made their necklaces, ask them to find a student who has a necklace of the same length but different-sized beads and to count how many beads each necklace has. Ask: How can you have the same length when you have more (fewer) beads?

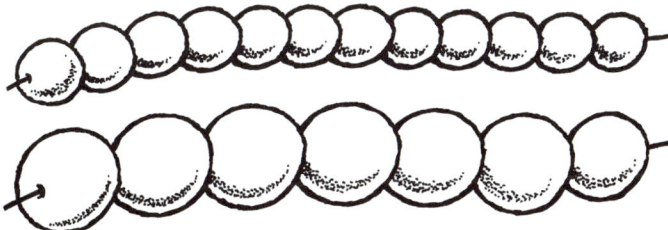

Covering a Surface

Build on 'Beads on a String' by using same-sized tiles (print shapes, leaves, foot prints, pattern blocks) to cover a surface. Invite students to count how many fit and describe the area by the number of units (e.g. *This is a 9-tile piece of paper.*)

SAMPLE LEARNING ACTIVITIES

Middle ✔✔✔

Snail Trails

Have students draw two 'snail trails', one 8 matchsticks long and the other 12 matchsticks long. Ask: Which trail is longer? How do you know? Ask students to remove the 12 matchsticks and replace them with enough popsticks to cover the line. Ask: How long is this trail now? Which trail is longer? How do you know? Discuss the idea that to compare two things we need to use the same size unit. (See Key Understandings 4 and 6, and Sample Lesson 1, page 32.)

Hungry Cow

Extend 'Desk Through the Doorway' by having students solve problems involving other attributes where direct comparison is not possible. For example, show students two different, irregular shapes of similar area drawn on one sheet of paper or card. Say: A farmer has these two paddocks on his farm. If you were a hungry cow, which would you prefer? Invite them to compare the two shapes. Ask: How can you compare the two paddocks? What could you use? Why do you have to use the same-sized object on both in order to compare? (See Key Understanding 5.)

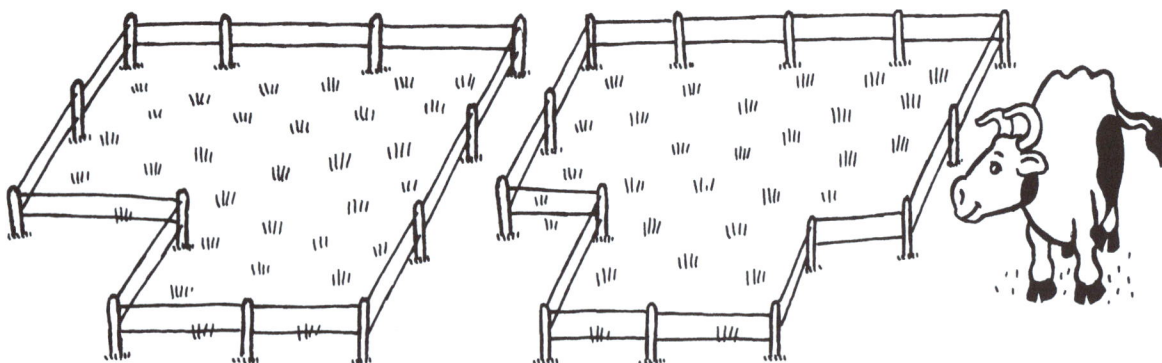

Steps

Have students measure and record distances around the school by walking and counting their steps. Ask: Does it matter whose steps are being counted? What happens if some of your steps are shorter than others? How could you be sure the distance to the office is the same as the distance to the library?

Body Measurements

Have students each choose an object to use as a unit to measure and record information about themselves (e.g. height, mass, distance around waist, length of arm, area of footprint). Ask them to compare their measurements with a partner and determine who is taller (has the greater mass, has the longer arm). Ask: What makes you certain you are taller (heavier) even though the number of units is less than your partner's? What have you chosen to use for your unit? How big is it? (Link to Key Understandings 1 and 2.)

One Popstick

Have students use one object repeatedly to measure. For example, to find out if a bookshelf will fit a given space, have students use one popstick, marking off and counting how many popsticks long the space is. Then, have them do the same with the bookshelf. Ask: Will the bookshelf fit the space? How do you know? Would you get the same answer if you matched the space with a line of popsticks? Why? Why not?

One Tile

Repeat 'One Popstick', but using one object to measure area. For example, during a science lesson, use one tile to say which of two different-shaped leaves has the larger area. Ask: What do you need to do with the tile to find out? Can you use that information to say how much bigger one is than the other?

Different Containers

Give pairs of students a large container, a selection of small containers and a bucket of water. Invite them to each choose a different small container to fill the large container. Ask them to take turns filling it with their container and say how many cups (lids, jars) they each took to fill it. When each student has counted and given their results, ask: How can that container be filled by three cups when you fill it and by five jars when your partner fills it?

Time Periods

Have pairs of students choose ways to measure short time periods without using a clock (e.g. counting claps, ball bounces, pendulum swings). Encourage them to use all the methods to measure the time taken to complete an activity (e.g. putting on their shoes, writing their full name, getting a drink). Have students compare results. Ask: How many pendulum swings did it take you to put your shoes on? How many ball bounces did it take? Why do you think you got a different result?

KU 3

SAMPLE LEARNING ACTIVITIES

Later ✔✔

Garden Plots

Have students decide on the attribute and the unit of measurement, in order to solve problems. For example, a school has two available pieces of land, one a rectangle and one a triangle, and wants to choose the largest one for a garden. Ask: Which one do you think is larger? What do you have to measure? What units of measurement will you use? Why? (See Sample Lesson 2, page 35, Key Understanding 1 and Direct Measure, Key Understanding 3.)

Comparing Gardens

Build on 'Garden Plots' by asking: How did you decide which garden was larger? Did measuring help? Use an actual example from the class or present a scenario; for example, say: Craig measured the triangular garden as 28 cubes and 6 green triangles and the square garden as 30 cubes and 4 cream rhombuses. He found it difficult to compare the gardens. Why? Why do we have to use the same unit for both shapes? (Link to Direct Measure, Key Understandings 3 and 5.)

Citrus Fruit

Have students use units to compare a range of attributes. For example, organise students into groups to decide which citrus fruit has the most juice. Invite each group to choose one type of citrus fruit and measure how much juice it has. Have various containers available for students to use as measures (e.g. cups, jugs, eggcups, teaspoons, lids). Encourage groups to compare their results with others to decide which type is the juiciest and by how much. Ask: Was it difficult to compare your results? Why do you think that happened? What decisions need to be made about the unit in order to easily compare the amount of juice? (Link to Key Understanding 4.)

Identikit

Have students choose suitable units to measure the volumes of different objects. For example, during the Later Sample Learning Activity 'Identikit' (Key Understandings 1 and 2), encourage them to tell their partner how they measured the volume of objects like a brick, an apple and a banana. For example, say: Some students used cubic centimetres and some used millilitres for the same object. How would they have done this and who is correct? Draw out the mathematical idea that volume can be measured using cubic units or liquid volume units.

Rectangles

Give pairs of students various rectangles with an area of 1 square metre (e.g. 1 metre by 1 metre, 50 centimetres by 2 metres, 25 centimetres by 4 metres) with which to measure the area of the same region, such as a pin board. Tell them that all their shapes have an area of 1 square metre. Have students record and compare measures. Ask: What do you notice? Does the shape of the object matter? Why? Why not? Draw out the mathematical idea that the unit we use to measure the area is a size. As long as that size stays the same, the shape doesn't matter. (Link to Direct Measure, Key Understanding 5.)

Racing

Organise students into pairs and have them decide on a time unit of some type (e.g. claps, ball bounces, counting, pendulum swings) to time each other racing over 50 metres. Invite them to record their 'best time' out of three and find out who is the faster of the two. Display the results on a class chart and stimulate argument by suggesting the class winner is the one with the lowest number (without accounting for the types of units used). Discuss ways that the given results could be fairly compared to arrive at the 50-metre 'champion'. Ask: How could we compare fairly? What would we need to do to find out how much faster the Olympic champion is for that length of race?

Treasure Hunt

Have students plan to hide four or five 'treasures' (e.g. sweets) around the school and write a list of measurement instructions for another pair to follow. Ask: What measurement information will you need to give for someone to find the treasure (the next clue)? How will they know how far to walk? How will they know what direction to walk in? How will you tell them how much to turn? Invite students to design their treasure hunt, place their treasures and then swap their clues with another pair to find the treasures.

Sorting Cards

Have students compare measures when the units of measurement are different. For example, prepare some cards showing a range of measures of length, area, volume or capacity and mass, in mostly different sizes (e.g. for length use millimetres, centimetres, metres and kilometres). Invite students to sort them into categories according to the attribute they measure. Then, in turns, have students take two cards from a category pile and say which measure is larger and why (e.g. which is larger out of 5 decimetres and 22 centimetres). Ask: Did you have to do anything to be able to compare the two measures? Were there measures you could compare without changing to the same unit? How did you order them? Shuffle the cards in each pile and repeat the activity. (See Key Understandings 5 and 8.)

KU 3

SAMPLE LESSON 1

Sample Learning Activity: Middle—'Snail Trails', page 28

Key Understanding 3: To measure something means to say how much of a particular attribute it has. We measure by choosing a unit and working out how many of the unit it takes to match the thing.

Teachers' Purpose

Students in Catherine's Year 3 class had begun to use units to measure length and seemed to be able to do it. For example, Roberto chose straws to measure the length of the bookcase and said, 'The bookcase is a bit more than twelve straws long'.

Catherine was not sure, however, whether they would use this information to compare the length of two different objects and decided that this should be the focus of her next measurement lesson.

Motivation and Purpose

Catherine provided sheets of paper on which she had drawn two straight lines to represent snail trails across a path. Each page was a little different, so students had to work with their own pair of trails.

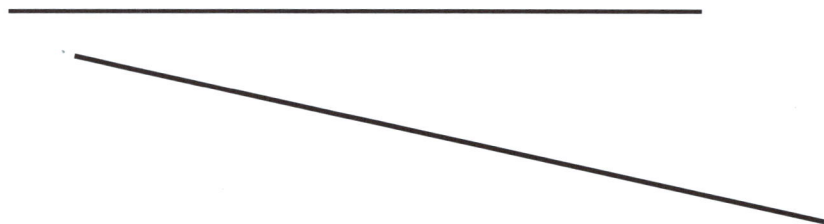

She gave each pair several different types of materials to use as units from among matchsticks, toothpicks, paper clips, marbles, blocks and beans, but made sure that there was only enough of any one material to measure one of the trails, not both. Catherine had a reason for doing this: she wondered if they *really* knew that the count was an indication of the length of the object. She didn't give them enough objects of the same size to match both lines at the same time because she wanted to create conflict that would provoke the students to think about what to do. Her goal was that they would work out that they could use the objects to measure one line, remember the number and then place the same objects onto the other line.

Catherine then asked, 'Which snail went further and how much further did this snail go than its friend?'

Action and Reflection

Almost all students began by choosing one of the units and repeating it by lining up the units end-to-end along the first trail. Many of them, however, happily chose a different-sized object (and hence unit) to measure the second trail. She saw Adam run out of matchsticks and begin using blocks that were a different size halfway along the second line. 'There wasn't enough, so I had to use another one.' After seeing what others in his group had done, he replaced the matchsticks on the second line with blocks.

Even though Catherine had anticipated that some students would choose to use different units, she was surprised that so few students thought about the need for the same unit and so did not feel any conflict about using different units. Having counted the units, most disregarded the object they'd used and simply compared numbers.

Catherine encouraged students to reflect on the sense of what they'd found. For example, Kim used matchsticks for the horizontal line and toothpicks (which were a different size to the matchsticks) for the other.

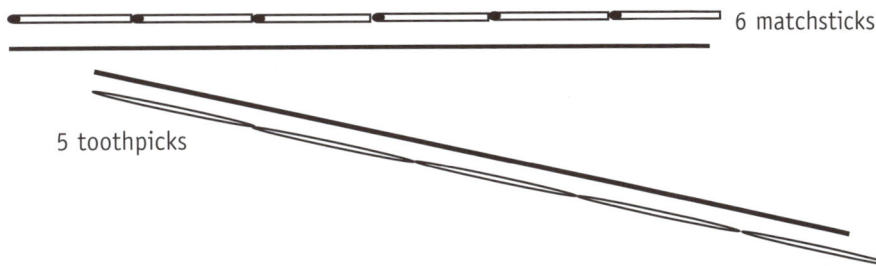

6 matchsticks

5 toothpicks

Catherine asked him why he chose the toothpicks. He said, 'They're skinny and they fit on the line better and I can see if they're straight on it.'

She then asked him which of his trails was longer and he immediately pointed to the diagonal line. Then, she asked, 'How much longer?'

Kim counted the units on each line, frowned, looked a bit confused, counted again and said, 'That's six, there's only five there, so it's one more?'

Catherine asked why he'd frowned and counted again. He said, 'I thought I was wrong because the five one's longer, but I counted again and it *is* one more there.'

> Catherine has helped Kim notice an anomalous or conflicting result without actually correcting him or simply telling him 'how to do it'.

Connection and Challenge

Catherine described what she'd found out at this stage:

> *I realised that Kim did not understand how counting the units related to the length. He carefully lined the units up end-to-end as I had taught*

him, but did not seem aware that the differing lengths of the two units would interfere with the comparison. He also ignored the 'part-unit' left on one line. His hesitation, however, suggested he might be ready to move on, so I suggested he try swapping the toothpicks and matchsticks over.

Kim did this and found that there were seven matchsticks and barely five toothpicks. 'Ah,' he said, 'It's two more, that has to be right—the long one's got more this time.'

He was clearly more satisfied with this result because the greater number agreed with his knowledge about which line was longer.

But Catherine wanted him to go further, and focused back on the type of units. 'So there's 7 *matchsticks* on the longer line, but how many *matchsticks* did you say fitted on the short line when you did it the other way?'

At this point, Kim paused, studying his trails intently, while Catherine waited. At last, he answered, saying, 'It was six.' But then he added in an excited voice, 'You don't need toothpicks, you just need matchsticks and then you don't get messed up, it's matchsticks on this line and matchsticks on that line and then it makes sense. It's 7 matchsticks on the long line and this one was 6 matchsticks, so the long line *is* more, it fits one more *matchstick*.'

Catherine had helped Kim begin to make a connection between the length unit and the attribute it measured.

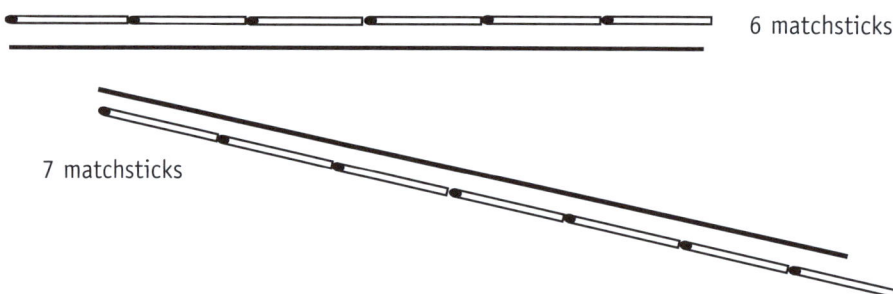

6 matchsticks

7 matchsticks

Drawing Out the Mathematical Idea

She gave Kim a different coloured felt pen and had him write down what he had found on his sheet of paper:

Catherine then paused and said slowly, 'So you are saying that this one is 6 matchsticks long but this one is 7 matchsticks (pointing) and it is the longer one. What about when you measure both with the toothpicks?' She left that with him!

Kim's confusion or concern about what he has found provides an opportunity for him to make a significant leap in his knowledge.

At this point, the nature of the teacher's input is crucial.

Catherine wants Kim to see that either the matches or the toothpicks could be used to make the comparison, but not both at the same time.

SAMPLE LESSON 2

Sample Learning Activity: Middle—'Garden Plots', page 43; Later—'Garden Plots', page 30

Key Understanding 3: To measure something means to say how much of a particular attribute it has. We measure by choosing a unit and working out how many of the unit it takes to match the thing.

Motivation and Purpose

I began by wanting to get my Year 4 students thinking about what sorts of things were useful for representing a unit of area. (See Key Understanding 4, Middle Sample Learning Activity 'Garden Plots'.) I asked them to compare two different-shaped garden plots and gave them a range of things to choose from to use to represent their unit, including matchsticks, 1-centimetre cubes, 2-centimetre cubes, pattern blocks, rice, counters and string.

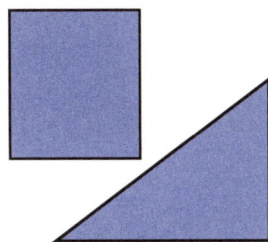

> Which garden plot has the most land? Choose the plot with the larger area so we can grow more vegetables on it.

The rectangle was exactly 11 centimetres by 12 centimetres so that 2-centimetre cubes would not fit exactly into it. The right-angled triangle was 17 centimetres by 15 centimetres. I chose regions that differed in area by just a few square centimetres so that the students could not say which was larger simply by looking and would have to find another way to compare them.

Connection and Challenge

When the students began work, I circulated, observing their strategies and asking questions. I noticed that a number of the students made their choice of measuring materials according to the shape of the region they were trying to measure and used different materials on one region than on the other. The idea of 'fitting' dominated their thinking. Joshua said, 'I've used blocks here, because it is a square and rice here because the blocks don't fit and rice fits better.' When I asked him if he'd found out which was larger, he just stared at his carefully placed blocks and rice for a few minutes, then looked at me rather helplessly and shook his head.

Other students, like Tilopa, used blocks on both regions, but filled in the gaps around the edges with rice. Asked which was bigger, she counted the blocks but had difficulty when she started to count grains of rice. Thus, some students did not see that using the same material on both regions would help them to make the comparison. Others saw this and started out using the same material for both regions but had difficulty with the gaps around the edges. I decided to focus on using the same material first (Key Understanding 3), rather than the gaps (Key Understanding 4 and Direct Measure, Key Understanding 3).

Action and Reflection

I stopped the students and asked, 'So, which region is bigger?'

Most agreed with Joshua, who said you could not tell. 'Why not?' I asked.

'Well,' said Joshua, 'you have to put different things on, blocks for the square and rice for the triangle.'

'Why did you have to use different things, Joshua?'

'Because they are different shapes, so some stuff won't fit on,' he replied.

'So what can we do to find out which is larger?'

I noticed earlier that Brendon used the same material on both but had difficulty covering the region with the materials provided. 'Brendon, did you find out which one was larger?'

'Well, sort of,' he said, 'I think the square might be bigger.'

'What makes you think that?' I asked.

'When I put blocks on both of them I had 30 blocks on the square and only 29 on the triangle. But the problem is that there was lots left over and so I couldn't tell really.'

'You managed to use blocks on both of them.' I said this because I wanted the students to begin to think about using the same material for both regions. 'Did anyone else cover both regions with the same thing?'

Halimah volunteered that she had used rice on both but could not tell which was bigger because it was too hard to count.

'But if you did count it, would you be able to tell which was the biggest?' I asked.

'Yes,' she said.

'So, how would you know which was biggest?'

'Because the one with the biggest number would be the biggest one. '

'So, why can't you tell which is biggest when you count what you have, Joshua?' I wanted the students to think about the importance of using the same unit on both regions.

'Because it is different when you have different stuff,' he said.

'I know,' said Tilopa, 'It's because they are not the same size. You see, rice is much smaller than blocks and so 30 pieces of rice is much smaller than 30 blocks.'

Drawing Out the Mathematical Idea

'Yes, that is important,' I said. 'You have to use the same thing on both of the shapes, otherwise you can't use the number to tell you which is bigger.'

I asked them to work with their partner to say what we needed to do, and then asked for a volunteer to say it to the class. I then repeated this for the whole class: 'Choose one type of material to use as your unit and cover both shapes with it. Count how many cover each shape. Then the numbers will tell which is bigger.'

They started the task again, all using the one material of their choice. I wasn't sure that all really understood the importance of using the same unit in order to compare, but they were on the way. I knew that many would experience the problem that Brendon and Tilopa had found, with fitting their units along the edges. This I would deal with later.

KEY UNDERSTANDING 4

The instrument we choose to represent our unit should relate well to the attribute to be measured and be easy to repeat to match the thing to be measured.

The focus of this Key Understanding is *choosing* appropriate things to use as units. It links closely with Key Understanding 3 in Direct Measure, which deals with the practical skill of *using* units well.

When we measure an object, we choose a unit and compare it with the size of the object, saying how many 'times as big' the object is as the unit. To say that an angle is 60°, for example, is to say that the angle is 60 times the standard angle we call 'a degree'. In practical measurement, we do this by selecting a thing to represent the unit and working out how many match or fit or balance the object. We ask questions such as the following.

- How many of these rods (units of length) fit along the table without gaps or overlaps?

- How many of these hexagons (units of area) cover my mouse pad without gaps or overlaps?

- How many of these cupfuls (units of capacity) fill our container fully without overflowing?

- How many of these marbles (units of mass) balance our teddy bear as well as possible?

- How many of these wedges (units of angle) match this turn as closely as possible?

- How many of these swings of the locket (units of time) does it take to walk across the room?

The thing we choose to represent our unit is our measuring instrument. Although all physical objects have attributes of length, area, volume, mass, angle, etc., they are not all equally helpful to use as units. Our choice can make accurate matching possible or impossible, easier or harder.

Firstly, the thing we choose to represent our unit should relate well to the attribute we are interested in. For measuring length, something long and thin is useful and it should be clear where it begins and ends. String is a useful instrument for measuring length, but it doesn't work well for measuring area. Paper triangles are good instruments for measuring area but, even though cotton wool balls have area, they are round and probably too easily squashed to make a good instrument.

Secondly, to make an accurate comparison, we have to squeeze as many of the units in as possible, but no more. We should, therefore, choose things to use as units that make it easy to match the object without gaps or overlaps.

Initially, students will use a wide variety of materials informally to represent their units—rods, leaves, paper clips, popsticks, marbles, potato prints, for example. Students who are through the Matching and Comparing Phase will think of the task of measuring as seeing how many of the chosen 'units' fit without too much concern for how well they fit. Over time, they will link their efforts to directly and indirectly compare objects with their capacity to work out 'how many fit'. They will see that working out 'how many fit' in each of two things can enable them to compare the two things indirectly. With appropriate experiences, they will come to see that if we repeat units to make as close a match as possible to each of two objects, the number of units needed in each case can be used to reliably compare the objects; that is, the number of units will tell us the size of each object. The importance of making a good match will be clear to them and they will see that some of these objects make the matching process easier than others.

Students who are through the Quantifying Phase will reject things that do not relate well to the attribute of interest when choosing something to represent the unit.

These students will also understand *why* gaps and overlaps are a problem and so will try to avoid them. They will, for example, choose shapes that tile to use as an instrument for area measurement and they see *why* it is important to line up the zero mark on the ruler with the start of the line to be measured.

SAMPLE LEARNING ACTIVITIES

Beginning ✔✔

Cupfuls, Pouring and Scooping

When students use cupfuls and scoops and pour from containers during their activities, focus on their choice of instrument to represent the unit. For example, ask: Will it be easier to use a large cup or a small lid to see how much an ice cream tub holds? (Link to Direct Measure, Key Understanding 3.)

Snail Trails

Give pairs of students a sheet of paper with two different straight lines on it representing snail trails. Invite students to choose a unit and say how many fit along each trail. Then, invite the class to sort out those that make as close a match as possible. Ask: Which unit will closely match the length, matchsticks or pens? Why? (See Key Understandings 3 and 6, and Sample Lesson 1, page 32.)

Using Balance Scales

Have students use balance scales and choose from different-sized marbles to match the weight of an object (e.g. a book, a block, a container). Invite them to work out which marbles make the closest match. Ask: Which marbles will match the weight of the object?

Prints

Invite students to cover a sheet of paper with prints using chosen objects (e.g. potato pieces, blocks) as stamps. Ask them to count how many they were able to fit in the region. Ask: Does it matter if they overlap? Can we use the number to say how big your sheet of paper is? At another time, repeat the activity and ask students to see if they can fit more stamps on this time without overlaps. Ask: Does it matter if they overlap? Can we use the number to say how big your sheet of paper is? (Link to Direct Measure, Key Understanding 3.)

Tracking Growth

Have students decide on a way to track the growth of bean shoots (wheat, carrot tops). Invite them to predict how much growth will take place each day and encourage them to choose objects small enough to be used as the unit (e.g. soaked blue boiling peas threaded onto sticks, linking centimetre cubes). (See Key Understanding 6.)

Balancing

In small groups, have students measure how heavy four pieces of fruit are. Have them use the balance scales and a unit of their choice (paper clips, cubes, marbles, string, bolts, rice, other pieces of fruit). Invite students to explain why they chose their particular unit. Have them compare what they chose with others. Ask: Which things were easier to get closer to balancing the apple? (See Key Understanding 5 and Direct Measure, Key Understanding 3.)

Paper Tiles

Have students cover different sides of a packing box with paper tiles to decide which side is bigger. Invite them to choose a unit from a range of different-sized tiles ranging from A4 to 2-centimetre squares. After they have counted the whole units, ask: Which sizes of paper meant you could cover more of the side? Which is best to use to say how big each side is?

Furthest Throw

Have students suggest different units to measure how far they throw a large ball. Ask: What do we want to measure? What shall we use? How will we do it? Take groups of students outside and invite them to try the different units. Ask: Of all the things you tried to measure with, which one was the best? Why? Have students record how far they throw the ball over a series of days. (See Key Understanding 6 and link to Estimate, Key Understanding 1.)

Measuring Everything

Organise students into groups and invite them to measure different things (e.g. height of a chair, time taken to do up their shoes, surface area of a desk, capacity of a container, weight of a book). Provide materials for measuring (e.g. straws, paper rectangles, paper triangles, cups, pendulums, string, stones, cubes). Encourage them to discuss suitable units for each type of measurement. Ask: What things were better for finding out how long it is (how much it holds, how heavy it is, how much of it is covered, how much time is taken)? Why?

Tapes

Have students make their own tape measures. Ask: Which things will help you to mark off units that are the same length each time? (e.g. a marble, a cork, a 1-centimetre cube, a matchbox, a piece of string). Why should you use one thing over and over? (Link to Direct Measure, Key Understanding 3.)

KU 4

SAMPLE LEARNING ACTIVITIES

Middle ✔✔✔

Which Object?

Ask: Which of these objects (e.g. length of dowel, carpet square, 2-centimetre cube) would help you find out who can fit the most in their lunch box (the amount of wallpaper needed to cover a wall, the height of a fence)? Ask students to justify their choices to the rest of the class. Draw out the mathematical idea that different objects are useful for measuring different things and have students explain why.

Suitable Objects

Following activities like 'Which Object?', have students brainstorm a list of objects that could be used to measure short lengths, long lengths, small areas, large areas, small volumes and large volumes. Ask: What makes an object suitable to use to measure a large area (small volume, long length)? (Link to Direct Measure, Key Understanding 3.)

Picture Frame

Have students choose an object to measure the distance around their artwork in order to make a frame. When they have measured their artwork, invite them to compare the objects chosen and explain why their object was useful for the task. Ask: What part of the object did you use to measure your artwork? Why did you use that part of the object? How many of your unit match the length needed for the frame? (See Direct Measure, Key Understanding 4.)

Units of Time

Organise students into groups and invite them to investigate which unit of time would be most suitable to measure different lengths of time (e.g. the age of a person, time taken to eat your breakfast, time taken for you to blink, length of time you are asleep, time taken to clean your room). Encourage students to discuss reasons for their choices. (Link to Key Understanding 5 and Indirect Measure, Key Understanding 4.)

Comparing Boxes

Have groups of students work out which box could hold more when comparing two empty boxes with slightly different volumes. Offer an assortment of materials, such as blocks, string, coloured rods, marbles, rice or beans. Ask: Which objects filled the boxes with no gaps? Which had the biggest gaps? Which objects best show the amount of space in the boxes? Why? (Link to Indirect Measure, Key Understanding 1.)

Garden Plots

Tell students that the school gardener can't choose between two plots to make the school herb garden. They look about the same size, but he wants to make sure he picks the one with the larger area. Give students scale drawings of the plots, one triangular and one rectangular. Ask them to find which is larger. Provide a range of materials to choose from to measure with (e.g. matchsticks, pattern blocks, tiles, counters, string, 1- and 2-centimetre cubes, rice). Ask students to explain why the object they chose was a good unit to use. (See Sample Lesson 2, page 35.)

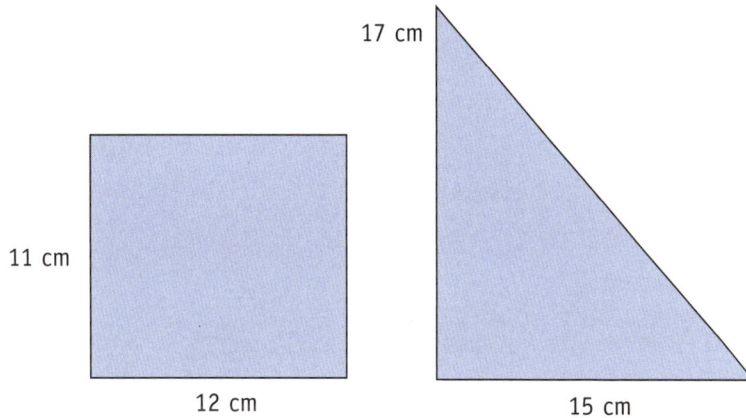

17 cm

11 cm

12 cm

15 cm

Spoonfuls

Have students use spoonfuls and cupfuls of rice (water) to measure the size of different containers. Ask: Does it matter that we have different measurements for the same-sized container? How has this happened?

Soft Toys

Ask students to use balance scales to weigh three soft toys to say how heavy each one is. Invite them to choose a unit from a selection of materials (e.g. marbles, washers, popsticks, wooden cubes, cottonwool balls). Ask: Why is it better to use the washers or marbles rather than the popsticks or cottonwool balls? (Link to Key Understanding 3.)

KU 4

SAMPLE LEARNING ACTIVITIES

Later ✔✔

Different Units

Organise students into groups and provide them with recipes and advertisements that show the units things are measured in (e.g. advertisements from supermarkets, newsagents and hardware stores). Encourage them to talk about why different ingredients and products are measured using different units. For example, ask: Why is sugar measured in kilograms and jam in grams? Why is a glue stick measured in grams and correction fluid in millilitres? Why is a cassette tape measured in minutes and ribbon measured in metres or centimetres? (Link to Key Understandings 6 and 7.)

Fruit and Vegetables

Have students compare the volume and surface area of vegetables (e.g. potatoes, carrots), using standard units represented by MAB materials and 1-centimetre grid paper. Encourage them to discuss the ways they can transform the objects so that the attributes to be measured can be more easily matched to the relevant units. For example, the potato can be carefully peeled and the pieces laid out on the grid paper to find the skin area. It can be cut and rearranged to approximate prism shapes that can be compared to the volume of MAB materials. (See Direct Measure, Key Understanding 3; link to Direct Measure, Key Understanding 5.)

Measuring Surface Area and Volume

Ask students to decide on appropriate units to use to measure the surface area of objects that are not rectangular (e.g. a circular garden bed) and the volume of objects that are not rectangular prisms (e.g. a heaped trailer load of sand). Ask: Which units do you think are best? Why do we use square units for objects that are not square? Why do we use cubic units for objects that are not rectangular prisms? (See Key Understanding 6; link to Direct Measure, Key Understandings 3 and 5, and Indirect Measure, Key Understanding 1.)

Choosing Units

Have students investigate the units that could be used to measure a variety of attributes (e.g. the mass and thickness of a £2 coin, the quantity of water in a bottle, the distance to the city, the capacity of a tablespoon, the capacity of an elevator (usually described in terms of mass), the amount of air inside a room). Encourage them to choose the units they think are most suitable for each measuring task and justify their choices.

Measuring Volume

Ask students to choose the most appropriate instrument to use to measure the volume of different objects. For example, ask students to measure the volume of a mug by immersing it in a measuring jug of water and recording the volume of the displaced water in millilitres. Then have them use a measuring jug to obtain the same volume of play dough and shape it into a cube. Invite them to compare the cube to MAB blocks and work out the approximate number of cubic centimetres it contains. Ask: What does this tell you about the amount of clay used to make the mug? How does the volume of one cubic centimetre compare to the volume of one millilitre? Have students measure volumes of other objects, justifying their use of either of the two instruments. (Link to Key Understanding 3 and Direct Measure, Key Understandings 2 and 5; see Did You Know?, page 86.)

KEY UNDERSTANDING 5

Measurements of continuous quantities are always approximate. Measurements can be made more accurate by choosing smaller units, subdividing units and other strategies.

While it is possible to count discrete quantities, such as people in a room or trees in a garden, continuous quantities, such as length, area and mass, cannot be counted. Instead, we measure such quantities by matching them against repetitions of a unit and counting the number of repetitions. Generally, the measurement is only as accurate as the unit. We might say, for example, that a pencil is 9 centimetres long. What we really mean by this is that the pencil is closer in length to 9 centimetres than to 8 centimetres or to 10 centimetres; that it is between 8.5 centimetres and 9.5 centimetres long. In this case, the possible 'error of measurement' is ± 0.5 centimetres. If we want to be more accurate, we use a smaller unit or subdivide the unit we have in some way. For example, we might measure the pencil with a ruler marked in millimetres.

Firstly, students should learn to describe their measures using 'between' or 'to the nearest' statements. They should say, for example, *the jug holds between 16 and 17 cups* or *the jug holds more than 16 cups but less than 17* or *the jug holds 16 cups to the nearest cup*. Technically, if cups are the unit, 'the jug holds 16 cups' means that the jug holds somewhere between 15.5 and 16.5 cups, but in many situations we would interpret 16 cups to mean 16 full cups. Students should discuss these contextual factors in how we describe measurements.

Secondly, students should develop strategies for making their measurements more accurate. A unit is a size, and the smaller the size, the more accurate the measurement. To choose a unit is, therefore, the same as choosing a level of accuracy. Students can be more accurate by choosing a smaller unit or subdividing a unit. For example, they could begin with a hexagon from a set of pattern blocks as their unit. Having decided they need something more accurate, they might choose the trapezium, which is half the hexagon.

Thirdly, students should understand that the object being measured doesn't change when you use a different-sized unit, although the number of units taken to match it will change—the smaller the unit, the more it will take to match the object. Students should therefore expect to find that twice as many trapeziums are needed as hexagons, since they are each half as big. This understanding is important in helping students to avoid the mistaken idea that a large number implies a large object, such as when they think that 2330 millimetres is a lot more than 1 kilometre.

Finally, students should subdivide units into parts and describe the parts using fractions and decimal numbers. For example, they might cut a strip of paper as their unit, and then subdivide it into quarters by folding. The strip could then be used to measure accurately to the nearest one-quarter strip. The relationship between the size of the units and the number of repeats needed is the basis for moving between units—that is, the same distance can be matched by 200 centimetre-units or by 2 metre-units—and hence relates closely to Key Understanding 8 about the relationships in the metric system.

Students who are through the Quantifying Phase will refer to the unit size to explain differences in the number of units taken. For example, they will explain that the reason Maria found the room was 16 strides wide but Jemmie found it was 14 strides wide was because Maria's stride was smaller.

Students who are through the Measuring Phase, understand the inverse nature of the relationship between the size of a unit and the number taken to match the object or event, and would expect that if you halve the unit size you will double the number of units.

Students who are through the Relating Phase, understand that choosing a unit is equivalent to choosing a level of accuracy, with the smaller unit producing the greater accuracy.

KU 5

SAMPLE LEARNING ACTIVITIES

Beginning ✔

Match Attributes

Ask students to count objects placed along (on, in) a larger object to describe the object in terms of how many things match its length (mass, capacity, area).

How Many

When students are focused on how many fit, and only use whole uniform units to cover an area with units (match the weight of an object using balance scales, match a given length, use cupfuls to say how much something holds), ask: Does it match it, or could more fit? How much more does it need? What could we do to make it the same area (weight, length, be full)?

Between

Have students match length, mass, volume, time and area with whole units and a part of the unit. For example, when students say how many pens fit along a desk, ask: If you could break this pen, how much of it would you need to make the pens match the length of the desk? Invite students to try this with toothpicks. Ask: How many toothpicks long is your desk? How much of a toothpick did you need to fit the gap at the end?

Silhouettes

Have students measure and record their height using popsticks as units. Ask pairs of students to make paper silhouettes of one another by drawing around one another in a standing pose (feet together) and cutting out the outlines. Ask them to fold the silhouettes in half lengthwise, count how many popsticks they can lie along the foldline from the baseline to the top of the head, and record their measurement (e.g. *I am more than 12 popsticks and less than 13 popsticks tall*). Order and display the silhouettes according to actual height. Ask: What do our popstick measurements tell us about the difference in our heights? What doesn't it tell us?

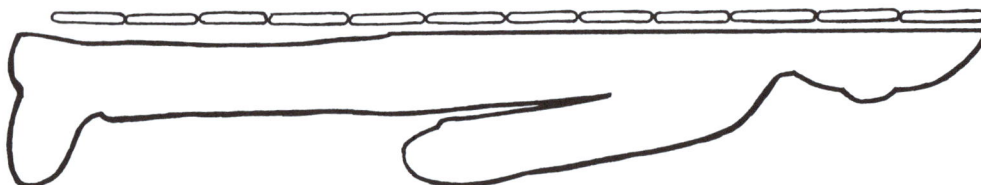

Full to Overflowing

Have students choose a cup from a collection of different-sized cups and use it to fill a clear tub as close to the top as possible. Ask them to record how many cupfuls they fit in before the next cupful will overflow, noticing the amount of space left before each cupful is poured in. Invite students to describe what they found. For example, *I put in two cupfuls and I thought there was lots of room for another one, but it overflowed. So it's more than two cups and less than three cups.*

Using Balance Scales

Have students use units of various mass to try to balance an object on balance scales. Ask them to look at and draw the slope of the balance beam before and after placing the unit that makes the mass of the units go from less than to more than the mass of the object. Ask: Which units changed the slope the most (the least)? Why? Invite students to think of something to use as a unit that would lessen the change in slope. (See Key Understanding 4 and Direct Measure, Key Understanding 3.)

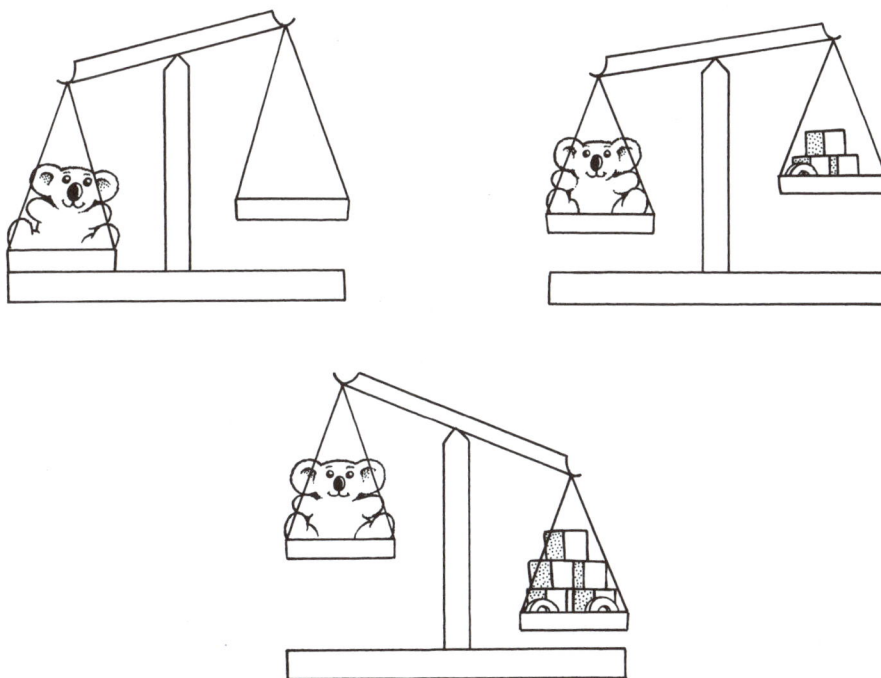

Tapes

Have students use the tape measures they made in Beginning Sample Learning Activity 'Tapes' (Key Understanding 4) to measure lengths around the room. Focus students on using half and quarter measures in order to be accurate. For example, if a students says: *It is 7 matchsticks long*, ask: Is that exactly right? Encourage students to mark the halfway point between the numbers to help.

KU **5**

SAMPLE LEARNING ACTIVITIES

Middle ✔✔✔

Feet

Ask students to draw around their foot, then repeatedly measure its length from heel to big toe using progressively shorter units (e.g. straws, popsticks, paper clips, pencil widths). Invite students to record the results using 'between' language on separate slips of paper for each unit type (e.g. *between 1 and 2 straws*). In groups, ask students to order their recorded foot sizes for each unit type. Ask: How does the ordering task change as the units get smaller? Why have you found there are fewer feet with the same measure as the unit gets smaller?

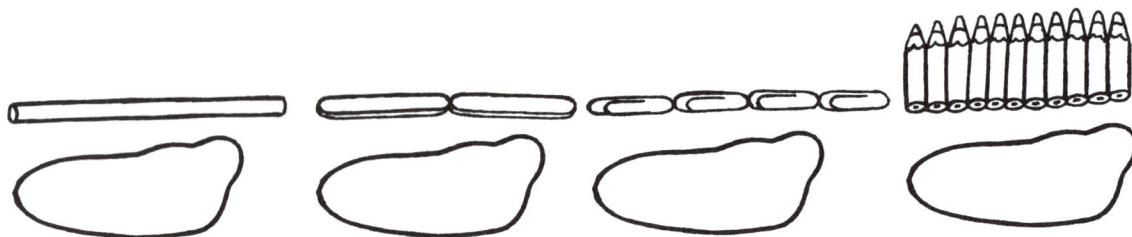

Balancing Hexagons

Have students use the hexagons from a set of pattern blocks as a unit of mass to balance with various objects (e.g. apple, book, rock, shoe), recording the result in hexagons. Invite them to repeat this, using other pattern block pieces to more closely balance the mass of the objects. Have them compare and discuss their results. Ask: How can this rock weigh both 12 hexagons and 25 trapeziums? What happens to the size of the number when we choose to use a smaller unit? (Make sure students have not mixed plastic and wooden pattern blocks in this activity.)

Smaller Units

Encourage students to explore the greater accuracy obtained when using smaller units in problem situations. For example, say: Mary used a cup measure and said the water bottle holds 5 cups. Jimmy used a half-cup measure and said the same water bottle holds 11 half-cups. Jimmy thought he must have made a mistake because 5 cups is equal to 10 half-cups, not 11. Both students were careful with their measurements, so how could this be? Does the volume of the container change when we use different units to measure it? Invite groups of students to use standard cup and half-cup measures to discover what happened.

Throwing Beanbags

Organise students into groups, giving each group a beanbag, a piece of chalk and a metre ruler. Take them outside and have each group measure how far they can throw a beanbag, starting from a baseline (e.g. on a basketball court). Ask them to mark their throws with chalk and measure them to the closest metre with the metre ruler. Order the measurements from shortest to longest. Ask: How could we be more accurate? Encourage students to choose either to subdivide the metre ruler or use smaller units, such as decimetres or centimetres. Ask them to remeasure the distances and reorder them. Ask: Why has it been easier to place our throws in order when we have used smaller units?

Hungry Cow

Extend Middle Sample Learning Activity 'Hungry Cow' (Key Understanding 3) by encouraging students to choose from a range of equipment, including cut out 1-centimetre squares and 2-centimetre squares, grid paper and clear plastic grids, to compare two different irregular paddocks of similar area drawn on one sheet of paper or card. Ask: Why is it easier to be more accurate using 1-centimetre squares than 2-centimetre squares? (See Key Understanding 3.)

KU 5

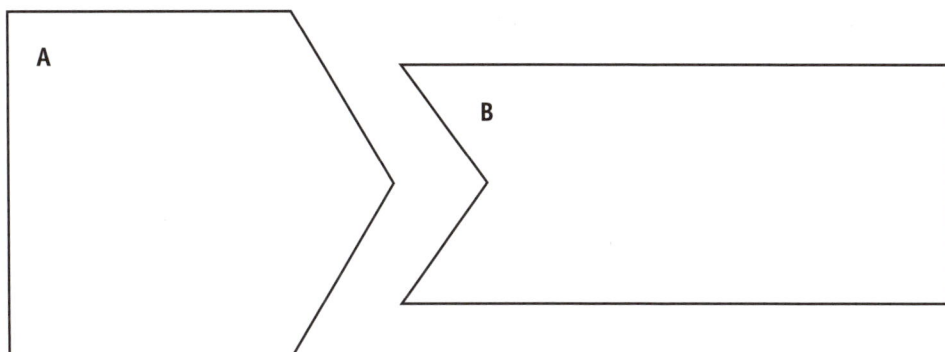

Note: The two shapes need to be on the same sheet of paper, so that direct comparison is not possible, and it should be very difficult to judge which is larger just by looking. For example, in the above, shape B looks smaller, but is 107 cm^2, while shape A is only 100 cm^2.

SAMPLE LEARNING ACTIVITIES

Later ✔✔✔

Body Measurements

Ask students to use equal strips (about 40 centimetres long) of unmarked paper to measure and record the length of different parts of their body, using the strip as a unit. Ask: Which parts of your body are equal in length? Invite them to talk about the problem this presents and find ways to make and describe part-units for their paper strips. Encourage students to explain and justify their choice of part-units. Ask: Can you measure the lengths accurately enough in part-units to know which parts of your body are equal in length?

Choosing Smaller Units

Have students choose smaller units to make measurements more accurate. Devise a task that takes a few minutes to complete and can be repeated. For example, ask: How quickly can you put 200 marbles, one at a time, into a plastic bottle? Who is fastest? Invite students to try the task, timing each other in minutes to find the winners. Minutes may be sufficient to compare the times at first (e.g. *nearly 3 minutes, just over 3 minutes, 3-and-a-half minutes*), but as students practise and become faster at the task it should become necessary to measure in seconds to differentiate between the fastest times. Draw out why greater accuracy was needed, and how using seconds as a unit provides it.

Calibrating Containers

Have students subdivide existing calibrations on a container to make it more accurate. Give groups identical jugs or containers, calibrated every 250 millilitres. Ask: Can you tell me what these marks mean? Have students use the measuring jug to say how much some smaller containers hold. Ask: Is the scale useful? Why? Why not? Then, have students use materials (e.g. small cone-shaped medicine cups, medicine spoons, ruler, disposable cups) to make a more accurate measuring tool. (Link to Key Understanding 7 and Direct Measure, Key Understanding 4.)

Sorting Cards

In pairs, ask students to sort cards that show a range of different measures and units into those that measure length, area, volume and mass. Have them take it in turns to take two cards from a pile and say which measure is larger and why (e.g. which is larger out of 5 decimetres and 22 centimetres, 0.3 litres and 0.375 millilitres, 2 hectares and 18-000 square metres, 3 kilolitres and 1245 litres). Say: Someone in the other class said that 18-000 square metres was bigger than 2 hectares. Are they correct? Why? Why not? Invite students to shuffle the cards in each pile and repeat the activity. (See Key Understandings 3 and 8; link to Direct Measure, Key Understanding 5.)

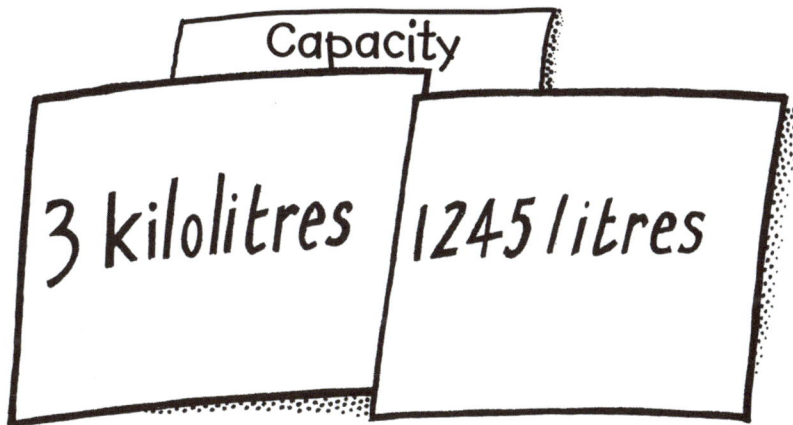

Overcoming Limitations

Have students explore strategies for obtaining accurate measurements of things that are too small for the measuring tools readily available to them (e.g. the thickness of a piece of paper, the mass of a single grain of rice, the volume of a drop from a eye dropper). For example, students could measure the mass of a teaspoon of rice, count the grains of rice and divide the mass by the number of grains of rice. Ask: What are we doing to the quantity of mass when we divide it by the number of grains? How is this similar to kilograms and grams? (See Indirect Measure, Key Understanding 4; link to *First Steps in Mathematics: Number*, Understand Operations, Key Understandings 3, 4 and 5.)

KEY UNDERSTANDING 6

Our choice of attribute and unit depends upon what we are trying to measure and why.

If students measure for a reason that is clear and of interest to them, then decisions about attributes and units are more likely to be made thoughtfully and be based on the purpose of the measurement and the practicalities of the situation. During the primary years, they should be encouraged to reflect upon and collaborate in making sensible choices about:

- which qualities need to be measured for the task at hand (attribute)
- how accurate they need to be for the purpose (unit).

In order to produce a scale drawing of part of the school garden, for example, students may decide that they need to measure various lengths and angles (attributes) and plan to be accurate to the nearest decimetre (unit) since the scale is to be 100 to 1.

Learning to choose the appropriate attribute links closely to Key Understanding 1. Students need to have a good understanding of what each attribute is and how they differ in order to be able to choose which attribute is needed in a particular situation. This is not always an easy task and students may not have the specific knowledge needed to consistently choose the right attribute. Nevertheless, they should experience a wide range of situations that require them to think consciously and carefully about what attributes need to be measured and should reliably choose the attribute for everyday situations.

Having decided what needs to be measured, students should then decide how accurate it needs to be. More accurate is not always better, sometimes it wastes time, over-complicates matters or makes calculations unnecessarily tricky.

The level of accuracy needed depends on the reason for measuring. Students often believe that the unit to be used depends only on the size of the thing to be measured. Sometimes the unit *is* related to the size of the things to be measured, but often it is not. A building may be measured with considerable precision (in millimetres) for detailed engineering work, but with less precision (metres) for estimating the amount of paint needed. To provide a quote for what carpet will cost for a large hotel, square metres may be sufficiently accurate and anything more accurate inefficient and spurious given the wastage involved. To cut the same carpet to fit a room, even a big room, more accuracy will be needed. If all you need to know is whether the cupboard will fit in the corner, hand spans may be sufficient. Choosing a unit is often iterative: where a bigger unit such as a hand span is used first and fairly quickly, if the things to be compared appear close in size, a smaller unit is then chosen and applied more carefully.

Students who are through the Quantifying Phase focus on relevant attributes to solve simple comparison problems that are familiar and meaningful to them. For example, they would focus on capacity when choosing the drink container that holds more and might show this by choosing a scoop or small container to act as a unit. They will choose suitable and uniform things to use as units.

Students who are through the Measuring Phase will choose units of a suitable size for descriptions and comparisons to be made. They will also select the attribute that is sensible for the purpose; for example, they would realise that even though we might consider the volume of cartons to see which would hold the most popcorn, dimensions would be more helpful for deciding which would hold the largest number of books.

Students who are through the Relating Phase understand the relationship between unit and accuracy and know that the unit chosen should make sense in terms of judgements about the importance of the measurement and the fineness of the comparisons to be made.

KU 6

SAMPLE LEARNING ACTIVITIES

Beginning ✔

Porridge for the Three Bears

Have students work in groups to decide on a container to serve porridge for the Three Bears. Baby Bear has a one-container serve, Mother Bear has a two-container serve and Father Bear has a three-container serve. Invite students to use the unit (container) to find a bowl the right size for each bear's porridge. Ask: Does the size of the container we use to make serves of porridge matter? Why? (See Key Understanding 3.)

Obstacle Course

Invite students to suggest ways to keep track of the time taken to complete an activity (e.g. clapping while someone completes an obstacle course). Ask: Do you think this is a fair way to keep track of time? Why? Why not?

Furthest Throw

Have students discuss how to find out who can throw the furthest. Ask: What could you do to find out? What would you need to measure? Would you measure how high or how far you could throw something? What could you use as units to measure that distance? Invite students to choose and try different units (e.g. popsticks, ropes, steps). Ask: Which of the things you tried to measure with made it the easiest to decide who could throw the furthest? (See Key Understanding 4.)

Snail Trails

Have students use glitter glue to make curved snail trails. Ask them to choose from a range of objects to use to measure how far each snail has travelled. Ask: What things can you fit along the curvy part of the trail? (See Key Understandings 3 and 4, and Sample Lesson 1, page 32.)

Tracking Growth

Extend Beginning Sample Learning Activity 'Tracking Growth' (Key Understanding 4) by asking: What part of the plant are we measuring? Is this its length (area, weight)? How do the peas help you know how much bigger the bean shoot (wheat, carrot top) is? (See Key Understanding 4.)

Weighing Small Animals

Ask students to decide what to measure to work out the size of a small animal (e.g. chicken, guinea pig). If they decide to measure its weight, provide a range of materials (e.g. blocks, marbles, washers) and ask them to choose what to use as units. Ask: What will we use to find out how heavy the chicken (guinea pig) is this week?

Ice-Cream Puddle

Have students choose from a wide range of materials to use for measuring tasks. For example, when working out the area of an ice-cream puddle, provide materials unrelated to area as well as materials that match it (e.g. rice, counters, blocks, paper tiles, paper clips, matchsticks, popsticks, balance beam, cups, lids, cottonwool balls). Ask: Which part of the ice-cream puddle are you measuring? Does your unit help you to measure this part? Would something else be a better unit? Why? Why not?

KU 6

SAMPLE LEARNING ACTIVITIES

Middle ✔✔

Travelling Cage

Say: I need to order a travelling cage for my cat. What will I need to know in order to buy the right cage? What would you measure to help me make my decision? What units would you use? How accurate would you need to be in your measurements? (Link to Key Understanding 1.)

Library Bags

Invite students to design a library bag. Ask: How big will the bag need to be? What measurements do you need to take? What unit size would be suitable? Why? How accurate do you need to be?

Shadows

Ask students to work with a partner to draw around the outside of their shadow in the morning, at noon and again later in the day. Invite them to describe how the shadow has changed. Ask: Will measuring the length be enough to decide which is the biggest shadow? Ask students to see if their morning and afternoon shadows have the same area. Ask: What unit size could you use to measure the area? Which one is the most suitable? Why? (Link to Indirect Measure, Key Understanding 4 and *First Steps in Mathematics: Space*, Represent Transformation, Key Understanding 3.)

Long Jumps

As a class, have students brainstorm all the ways they could measure long jumps for a competition. Ask: How accurate does the measurement need to be? How important is it? Discuss what would be an appropriate unit size (e.g. metres, paces) and instrument to represent the unit (e.g. metre rule, popsticks, tape measure). Would it be any different if you were judging the long jump at the Olympics? Could this unit be used to measure the high jump as well? (Link to Key Understandings 7 and 8.)

Juice

Have students decide how much juice will need to be bought for a school excursion. Ask: What will you need to know? What will you need to measure? How accurate do you have to be? What units would be sensible to choose? Will it matter if there is too little or too much? (Link to Indirect Measure, Key Understanding 4.)

Paperweight

Have students design a paperweight to hold down paper when the fans are on high (when the doors and windows are open, when they are working outside). Have them decide on a unit of weight that most of the students will be able to use (e.g. marbles, washers). Once they have worked out how many washers (marbles) in weight are needed to hold down the paper, ask them to write a memo to other classes to say how heavy the paperweight needs to be. (See Key Understanding 7.)

Units of Time

Ask students to choose an appropriate unit of time to say how long each of a number of activities takes (e.g. eating an apple, growing beans to get a pod, flying to Uluru or Antarctica, walking a kilometre, running 500 metres at the Olympics, flying to the moon, a person's lifespan, building a pyramid). Ask: Which instruments are used to measure the different units and why? (Link to Direct Measure, Key Understandings 4 and 6.)

KU 6

SAMPLE LEARNING ACTIVITIES

Later ✔✔✔

Lawns and Garden Beds

Say: The gardener needs to put new kerbing around the garden beds and fertilise the lawns. How will she work out how much curbing and fertiliser she needs? What will she measure? Invite students to determine which attributes need to be measured (perimeter and area) and decide on appropriate instruments and units to use. Ask: What unit have you chosen to use for the area? Why? What unit have you chosen for the perimeter? Why? Encourage them to justify their choice of unit size in relation to the level of accuracy required. (Link to Key Understanding 5.)

Classroom Furniture

Ask students to draw the classroom and its furniture to scale to use as a basis for creating some alternative floor plans. Establish the scale as 1 metre equal to 1 centimetre. Have them measure their desks and work out dimensions for the scaled drawing. Ask: Would you measure your desk to the nearest millimetre? Would you measure it to the nearest centimetre? Why? Why not? Which unit would you choose? Why would decimetres be a sensible choice for the purpose of your plan? (Link to Indirect Measure, Key Understanding 3.)

Carpet and Paint

Have students decide which measurements are needed to work out how much carpet and paint would be needed for the classroom. Ask: What should we measure so that sufficient carpet and paint are ordered? What will the carpet layer and the painter need to know? Organise students into groups and give them carpet advertisements and labels from paint tins to help them decide. Ask: Why would the painter need to know the area of wall to be painted, even if the school supplies the paint? (Link to Key Understanding 1 and Indirect Measure, Key Understanding 4.)

Measurement Situations

Have students build up a list over time of measurement situations; for example, working out how much juice to order for a class picnic (cough syrup for a toddler, cherries for a fruit salad, bricks for a barbecue area). For each situation, ask students to decide what they will measure, which unit and what tool they will use. Encourage them to justify the size of the unit they have chosen in terms of the accuracy needed. Ask: Why do some situations require a very small unit to measure a large object? (bricklayer building a house, weedkiller garden spray) (Link to Key Understanding 5.)

Measuring Surface Area and Volume

Vary Later Sample Learning Activity 'Measuring Surface Area and Volume' (Key Understanding 4). Ask students to choose the attribute, unit and instruments to measure the area of objects that are not rectangular (e.g. garden bed, orange) and the volume of objects that are not rectangular prisms (e.g. trailer load of sand, wet cement). Encourage students to consider a range of purposes. For example, for a circular garden bed, ask: How will your measurements vary if you want to find out how many rose bushes to plant and how much mulch to buy? What about if you want to find out how much fertiliser to spread? Do you need to know the dimensions or the area or volume? Which units are best to use? Why can we use square metres for a garden that is not square? Why can we use cubic units for objects that are not prisms? (Because they measure size, not shape.) (See Key Understanding 4; link to Direct Measure, Key Understandings 3 and 5, and Indirect Measure, Key Understanding 1.)

KU 6

Treasure Hunt

Extend the Later Sample Learning Activity 'Treasure Hunt' (Key Understanding 3) by asking students to redesign their instructions and adjust their units according to how successful their instructions were. For example, ask: Why might you need to give your measurements in metres rather than steps? How could you describe a turn that is between a quarter turn and a half turn? Would another unit be more useful? (See Key Understandings 3 and 6; link to Direct Measure, Key Understanding 3.)

Later ✔✔✔

Track and Field

Invite students to look at track-and-field title holders and their record times or distances for the various events. Discuss the relationships between the distances and the level of accuracy required of the units and the tools needed to measure them. For example, ask: How accurate would you need to be to tell who won a marathon (1500-metre race, 100-metre race)? Have students simulate the possible 'winning margins' (e.g. have them touch the wall one hundredth of a second after their partner) using available measuring instruments. Have students research the winning margins for Olympic distance events (e.g. shot put, javelin, long jump, high jump). Ask: Why is a dead heat more likely in high jump than long jump? (the high jump bar is raised in fixed increments) (Link to Key Understandings 5 and 8.)

Birth Weights

Have students bring in their birth weights in grams. Help them to compare their weights to the same mass measured to the nearest 100 grams and to the nearest kilogram by listing them in a table with those headings. Ask: Why does the difference between your birth weights appear to change when larger units are used? Why would babies be measured in grams while older children and adults are measured in kilograms or half kilograms? (See Sample Lesson 3, opposite, and Key Understanding 7.)

SAMPLE LESSON 3

Sample Learning Activity: Later—'Birth Weights', page 62

Key Understanding 6: Our choice of attribute and unit depends upon what we are trying to measure and why.

Teacher's Purpose

My Year 6 students were using bathroom scales to record their mass to the nearest kilogram and comparing the way their mass was recorded at birth with their current mass. I asked why their birth masses were 'more' than their current mass; for example, 'Katie's birth weight was 3254 grams, and now she's only 38 kilograms!'

They laughed and were able to say their mass was actually a lot more now, the 'thousands' is because their birth mass was grams and their mass now is kilograms, showing they understood grams were much smaller units than kilograms.

When I asked, 'Why weren't you measured in kilograms when you were born?', however, Jemina said, 'You can't, because babies are tiny, you have to be bigger to be kilograms.'

Others nodded in agreement. Although they were partly right in thinking that the size of the object to be measured was relevant, I was not convinced that they understood that the real issue was how accurate you needed to be. For people of adult size, a kilogram or half kilogram is usually accurate enough for practical purposes, but it would not be accurate enough to track weight changes in babies.

Action ...

The following day, I brought in some spring scales. The scales were calibrated to 100 grams and had every 500 grams written in, as well as the kilograms. I started by having students make up their birth weights (brought in from home) in MABs, using either gram weights and balance scales, or the school's digital scales that measured to the nearest gram. The next step was to weigh each child's 'birth mass blocks' on the spring scale. Each child took it in turns to place their blocks on the spring scales, while the rest of the students worked out the weight to the nearest 100 grams.

KU 6

The student selected to call out the weight had to justify it by showing how the pointer had to be one side or the other of an imagined halfway mark. The measurements were recorded on a wall chart beside the gram measures.

Students were then asked to weigh their collection of blocks on the bathroom scales in the same way they'd weighed themselves before—to the nearest kilogram—and record this as well. All this information was added to another column on the chart.

Name	Birth mass Measured to the nearest		
	gram	100 grams	kilogram
Katie	3264	3 kg 300 g	3
Ariel	3235	3 kg 200 g	3

... and Reflection

In a follow-up session, we looked at the chart together and talked about what was different about the measurements of their recorded birth weight and the measurements of the blocks done on the two types of scales.

Ariel observed, 'They're all kind of the same thing but sort of different—the first grams [the hospital-recorded masses] are kind of closer to the real thing, but after that it's like nearly, but not exactly.'

Katrina noticed that by measuring their simulated birth mass (blocks) to the nearest kilogram, different birth weights now looked the same. 'If you look at the kilograms when we were born, most everyone was about three kilograms, but if you look at the grams, everyone looks different.'

Connection and Challenge

I then asked, 'If Katie and Ariel actually had been weighed at birth, using the 100-gram unit on the spring scale, what would you have thought the difference in their weight was?'

The students responded they would have thought the babies had a difference of 100 grams in their weight. I followed on by asking, 'Did the babies really have a difference of 100 grams at birth?'

The students took a while, but most then thought 'no'. Katrina said, 'If you look at the column where they are measured in grams, there is only about 30 grams difference between them.'

I then asked a series of questions, 'Which is the most accurate measure? Why do you think so? Which was the least accurate measure? Why do you think so?' The students' responses made me think that they were starting to get the idea that the size of the unit affected the accuracy of the mass measure.

The smaller the unit, the more accurate the measurement. So if we need to be more accurate we choose a smaller unit.

Drawing Out the Mathematical Idea

I then turned to the question of why you might want more accurate information for babies than adults. I asked, 'So why do you think the babies were measured in grams and not kilograms?'

Quite a few students made comments like, 'when you need to be really right', 'when it's important to be accurate' and 'when you need to know the difference between things that weigh nearly the same, a kilogram is too big'.

I picked these ideas up and talked a little about how a difference of a few hundred grams can be quite a lot for a new baby. 'We often want to check whether the baby is losing or gaining weight and the amounts will be small. For adults, variations of under a kilogram are usually not very significant.'

To emphasise that it wasn't simply the size of the baby that was the issue, I also talked with them about adults who had eating disorders or other illnesses and the need at times to monitor small variations in weight.

They seemed to understand that the need to make fine distinctions (that is, to compare things that are close in size) means you need to be more accurate and hence need to use smaller units.

> *To decide how accurate we need to be we ask these questions:*
> - *How close in size are the things we want to compare?*
> - *How important is it that we get a close match between measurements?*

KU 6

? *Did You Know?*

In *Gulliver's Travels* (Jonathan Swift), Gulliver was twelve times as tall and wide as the Lilliputians. The Lilliputians worked out that Gulliver's mass would be related to his volume and that his volume would be 12 x 12 x 12 the volume of a Lilliputian. (See Indirect Measurement, Key Understanding 2.) So they gave him 1728 times as much food. The Lilliputians got their arithmetic right, but not their biology. The amount of food a person needs is related to heat loss, which is why the food value is given in kilojoules (or calories), and heat loss is related to surface area. Hence, Gulliver only needed 144 times as much food as the Lilliputians. Jonathan Swift chose the wrong attribute. Choosing the right attribute requires more than mathematical knowledge, it requires *numeracy*, that is, the intelligent blending of mathematical and contextual knowledge.

KEY UNDERSTANDING 7

Standard units help us to interpret, communicate and calculate measurements.

Initially, young students will use standard units in much the same way they use non-standard units. As they mature, they should come to understand the usefulness of standardising some units for recording and communication purposes. They should learn to distinguish between situations in which non-standard units may be used and situations where a standard unit would help. In particular, they should learn the following:

- Standard units are no more correct or accurate than non-standard units. A matchstick will give a more accurate measure of the side of a table than will a 1-metre strip.

- Non-standard units may be appropriate to and practical for the task at hand. Hand spans may be quite good enough to let you see how far a table will jut into a room.

- Some units are in common use, but are not standardised. These units may be more variable, regional and trade- or craft-specific, but be of local practical use. Three barrowfuls of sand will communicate well and be reliable within specific contexts.

- When measurements must be recorded for later use, transported or communicated, it helps to use units that are remembered over time and that other people share. Standard units are useful for this.

- In order to interpret other people's measurements, it is necessary to know their units; for example, we do not know whether 38 is a hot day or a cold day until we know what the unit is.

- To add, subtract and average measurements, it is necessary to use the same unit. Standard units help when measurements are collected by different people at different times (e.g. birth weights).

- Some formulas that show the relationship between quantities depend upon the units of measurement. Without standard units, we could not always use each other's formulas.

Students should learn about how various cultures have developed different units of measure, both historically and presently, and that the use of the metric system of measurement is becoming increasingly widespread. The basic metric units are metre, litre and kilogram, with other units being derived from these.

Students who are through the Quantifying Phase understand that to compare two measurements it is necessary to use the same unit and that the units they choose will often be standard simply because they are readily available in useable forms. Those who are through the Measuring Phase use standard units naturally in their own comparisons and communications. Students who are through the Relating Phase, can explain the roles of standard units but also recognise situations where a standard unit is not an advantage. They understand that the fact that a unit is standardised does not make it more accurate than other units; accuracy relates to unit size.

KU 7

SAMPLE LEARNING ACTIVITIES

Beginning ✔

Naming Units

Informally introduce the names of standard units when the opportunity arises. For example, as students play in a class shop, say: That jar weighs 250 grams. That tells us how heavy it is. When students read the numbers on a ruler, say: They are centimetres. We can use centimetres to tell us how long something is.

Measuring Jugs

When students make a measuring jug to use in their activities by cutting the top from a clear plastic bottle and calibrating it in 'cups', give them containers showing standard units (e.g. medicine and cooking cups and spoons, jugs, litre bottles, packets). Ask: Is your cup measure the same as a cup measure in the recipe books? Does it matter that they are different? Why? Why not? What is a standard cup measure in England? (See Direct Measure, Key Understanding 4.)

Measuring Lengths

Ask students to measure small lengths (e.g. the side of a book, a pencil) by counting centimetre cubes, then by using strips of centimetre-grid paper. Discuss the advantage of writing the numbers on the grid paper, so it is not necessary to count every time. When students are proficient using their grid paper tape, ask them to line up the marks on their ruler with those on the paper. Draw attention to the extra bit of wood or plastic left on each end of the ruler and the zero label at the starting point. Ask: Where do you start measuring from when you use the ruler? (Link to Direct Measure, Key Understanding 4.)

Class Shop

Have students set up a class shop as a permanent part of the classroom for a period of time. Organise them into groups and invite them to make the products the shop will sell. Ask them to label the packages with signs that indicate the size of the containers or the quantity of the contents. Help students find and copy the information from the packaging. Have a variety of different weights of, say, 250 grams, 500 grams, 1 kilogram and 2 kilograms and different capacities of, say, 250 millilitres, 500 millilitres, 1 litre and 2 litres. Encourage groups of students to use the shop, serving, making purchases, ringing through or writing down their orders.

Tools for Measuring

Make a class collection of different tools for measuring length (e.g. tapes, rulers). Invite students to say what they notice about the size of the gaps between the marks (e.g. *They're all the same size. Some are long and some are short.*) Ask: There are long marks and short marks. What do you notice about where the long marks are? Why aren't all the marks the same lengths? Invite students to choose a measuring tool and measure a given set of small objects (e.g. box, block, pencil) by counting the number of units (gaps), then compare their results. Ask: Why do you think you all counted the same number even though you used different tools? Discuss the name of the standard unit on the tool.

Stories of Units of Measure

Read and tell stories (e.g. *Noah's Ark, The Elves and The Shoemaker, The Emperor's New Clothes*) that mention standard units the characters of that time and culture used to measure things. Ask: What did Noah use to measure the ark? (cubits) What could the shoemaker have used to measure the leather? What could the tailor have used to measure the cloth?

KU 7

SAMPLE LEARNING ACTIVITIES

Middle ✔✔

Jack's Hand Spans

Present scenarios for students that deal with the reasons for using standard units. For example, say: Jack wanted to make a ramp for his toy cars. He phoned the local hardware store and asked if they stocked planks that were 10 hand spans long. What do you think the owner said to Jack? If Jack went to the store, how could he make sure he got the right-sized plank? What would be another unit for Jack to use? Can you think of a situation where hand spans could be suitable? Why?

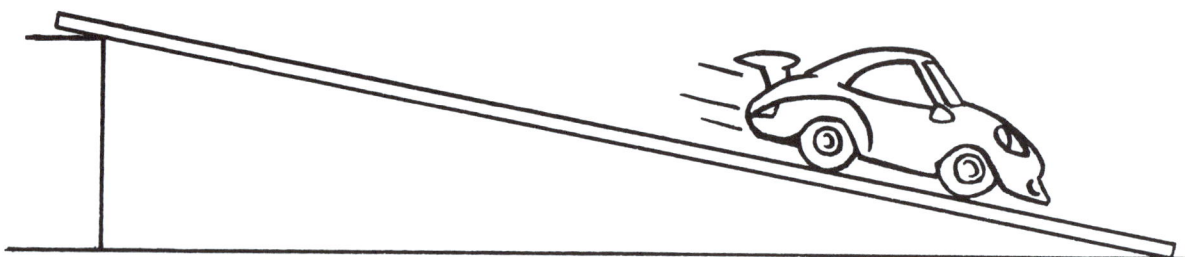

Units from Other Times and Cultures

Have students use books such as *Measure Up* (Meredith Costain and Marjorie Gardner, Ashton Scholastic) to research how standard units from other times and other cultures arose and what they were based on. Invite students to re-create these other standard units and use them to measure. Ask: Why do you think units such as the span and cubit are no longer used?

How Much Ice Cream?

Have students work in groups to decide how much ice cream would be needed for a special school lunch, using a non-standard unit such as spoonfuls or cups. Ask: What size container will we need to buy? What unit of measure is on the container? Why are measurements always on things sold in the supermarket?

Tee-Ball

Before students play a game of tee ball, have them research to find out how far apart the bases should be. Ask: Why is this written in metres and not as the number of steps? Invite students to lay out the bases using the measurements and then work out how many steps apart the bases are. Ask: Do we need to use the metre measure each time we play tee ball, or are steps accurate enough? Why?

Cooking

During a cooking activity, have students compare the sizes of different cups before using them. Ask: Does the size of the cup matter? Why? Ask students to find out how much a cup commonly holds in recipe books.

Birth Weight

Have students find out how much they weighed at birth. Record the information and focus on the use of the two different units, pounds and kilograms. Ask: What is the difference between the two units? Why are both units used for birth weight? Can you think of other times where standard non-metric units are used in the community? (e.g. *He's over 6 foot*, *It's miles away*.) (See Key Understanding 6.)

Paperweight

Extend Middle Sample Learning Activity 'Paperweight' (Key Understanding 6) by asking: How can you be sure that the measurements are accurate? Would the weight of the paperweight be the same if gram and kilogram units were used? Why? Why not? (See Key Understanding 6.)

KU **7**

SAMPLE LEARNING ACTIVITIES

Later ✔✔✔

Maths at Work

Invite speakers (parents) in to talk about the measurements they use at work, or show videos that describe how measurement is used in various occupations. Have students record the types of measures that are used in these different places of work (e.g. building sites, weather bureaus, airports, hospitals). Ask: Which of these units are standard and which are non-standard units? When would it be acceptable to use non-standard units? (e.g. using wheelbarrows as a measure for the amount of mortar needed in bricklaying) When would using a non-standard unit be inappropriate? (e.g. measuring the length of the brick wall to be laid)

Birth Weight

Extend the Middle Sample Learning Activity 'Birth Weight' by asking: How much weight have you gained since birth? Invite students to use bathroom scales to determine their current mass in kilograms and compare this to their birth mass to find the difference. Ask: What did you have to do to compare? How easy (difficult) was it? Why? (See Key Understanding 6.)

Comparing Standard and Non-Standard

Have students each make a tape measure using a non-standard unit of their choice (e.g. straw, popsticks, pens). Ask them to make the tape ten units long (a deca-unit) and subdivide it accurately into deci-units and centi-units. Invite students to use their tape to measure and cut a paper streamer to fit across a cupboard or window. Invite them to then use a standard metric tape to measure and cut a second streamer to fit the same space. Ask them to compare the two streamers. Ask: Why is there is little or no difference in the two lengths? Why are standard units used if there is no difference in accuracy?

Measuring Time

Have students research how the daily rotations of the earth, the monthly changes of the moon, and our planet's yearly orbits about the sun provided some of the first units for measurement of time. For example, Egyptians were the first to divide the day into 24 units and daylight into 12 units; the Chinese divided the whole day into 12 units; early Hindu civilisations divided the day into 60 units. After reviewing the different historical methods, invite groups of students to devise a new basis for measuring time, defining the set of units they need and justifying their choices.

Overseas

Students research (e.g. by looking at catalogues on the Internet, investigating the packaging of items) the way items are measured in Australia and in other countries (e.g. nails, hats, shoes, gloves, shirts, dresses, trousers, paper, knitting needles, wire, concrete, rainfall, television screens, bricks, ice cream). Display the items, or pictures of the items, and label them with the measurements as they become known. Encourage students to discover the origin of the various systems and units used and identify those based on the metric system. Explain the difficulties that might arise when the systems are not standardised between countries.

Travelling Overseas

Extend 'Overseas' by having students research standard units used in other countries. Ask: What are some of the problems a traveller might face? What might be confusing? (e.g. working out how fast you can drive, following recipes, using electrical appliances).

SI Units

Have students find out which SI (Standard International) units the UK and Europe uses and what the standards are for these units. Build up a list of basic units and the units derived from them. Have students research the units used in Australia before the change to metric. Ask: Which units are still used? (miles, feet, inches, pounds, pints) What are their metric equivalents? Why might people continue to use the old units? Provide some American magazines and ask students to list all the measurement words they can find, then compare them to UK units for the same attribute, before and after the change to metric. Ask: Which are the same and which are different? Why are communities often reluctant to change their standard measurements?

Units from Other Times and Cultures

Extend Middle Sample Learning Activity 'Units from Other Times and Cultures' by asking: Why do you think the UK decided to change to the metric system? What were the advantages (disadvantages) of the change? Have students interview people old enough to remember the change to metric measures. Ask: Was it difficult for them? How? Why?

Pre-Christian Dates

Have students research some famous people from the pre-Christian era and list the birth and death dates given. Ask: Would these have been the dates given at the actual time? Have students attempt to discover the way these events could have been recorded in their place and time and the units of time they used.

KU 7

KEY UNDERSTANDING 8

The relationships between standard units in the metric system help us to judge size, move between units and do calculations.

The metric system has all the features of decimal place value built into it and understanding it relies on understanding the multiplicative relationships between the places in decimal place value (see *First Steps in Mathematics: Number*, Whole and Decimal Numbers, Key Understandings 7 and 8). It is this that makes the metric system so useful. Conversions based on tens require only the movement of the decimal point (such as changing 34.56 kilometres to 34·560 metres) and so is more straightforward than those based on other numbers. The comparison of measurements is also easier. For example, even if we had never seen a litre or millilitre, we can compare 0.4 litres with 250 millilitres because we know that milli *always* means 'one thousandth' and so 250 millilitres must be 0.25 litres which is less than 0.4 litres. This also helps us to make judgements of relative size for measures of which we have little personal experience. Knowing how much a litre is, we also know how much a kilolitre is—it is 1000 times as much. This can help us get a sense of measurements outside our direct experience: big distances or very small masses.

Often students learn the relationship between particular units of measure (e.g. that 10 millimetres is equal to 1 centimetre, and that 100 centimetre is equal to 1 metre) as though they were unrelated 'facts'. The benefit of the metric system is that the same set of multiplicative relationships is built into all metric measures through the prefixes; having learned the relationship for one attribute, you know them for all attributes and the same decimal structure can be used for all measures.

kilo-unit	hecto-unit	deca-unit	**unit**	deci-unit	centi-unit	milli-unit
1000 units	100 units	10 units	**1 unit**	$\frac{1}{10}$ unit	$\frac{1}{100}$ unit	$\frac{1}{1000}$ unit
thousand	hundred	ten	**one**	one tenth	one hundredth	one thousandth

In the context of helping students understand metric units, it is also important that they recognise which of our units do *not* use decimals; for example, time and angle (degrees).

(In the Imperial system, conversions between units were unrelated to each other; that is, we had 12 inches in a foot, 3 feet in a yard, 16 ounces in a pound, 14 pounds in a stone, and so on. This meant that each relationship had to be memorised separately and calculations were complex. If we teach students metric relationships and conversions in the same way we would have taught conversions for Imperial units, we have withheld from them the very advantages the metric system brings.)

Did You Know?

The abbreviations for metric units are simple to derive. They are formed by joining a prefix abbreviation to a base unit abbreviation.

For example, 2 *kilograms* is written as 2 *kg* (*k* for *kilo* and *g* for *gram/s*), 2 *decilitres* is written as 2 *dL* (*d* for *deci* and *L* for *litre/s*) and 2 *decametres* as 2 *dam* (*da* for *deca* and *m* for *metre/s*).

For area and volume units, the abbreviation for the length unit is used and ^{2} is added for square units and ^{3} for cubic units. For example, 2 *square kilometres* is written as 2 km^2 and 2 *cubic centimetres* as 2 cm^3.

Prefix abbreviations		Base unit abbreviations		
kilo	k	length	metre/s	m
hecto	h	capacity	litre/s	L
deca	da	mass	gram/s	g
deci	d			
centi	c			
milli	m			

Some naming exceptions for metric units that students are likely to encounter are the hectare (ha), which is equal in area to a square with sides measuring 100 metres (or 10 000 m^2), and the tonne (t) which has a mass of 1000 kilograms.

KU 8

SAMPLE LEARNING ACTIVITIES

Beginning ✔

Metric Measurements

Incorporate metric measurement terms such as kilometres, litres and kilograms into stories and instructions for imitative play (e.g. in the sandpit, or in the class shop). Sometimes refer to milk cartons as litre containers, margarine tubs as 250-gram containers and rulers as 30-centimetre rulers.

Class Shop

Extend Beginning Sample Learning Activity 'Class Shop' (Key Understanding 7) by discussing standard units as students use the shop to draw out the relationship between standard units in the metric system. For example, say: Sam bought a litre of milk; Carla bought 600 millilitres. This means Sam has more milk because litres are much bigger than millilitres.

Deca-Units

Ask pairs of students to choose one of the various units of measurement they have been using (e.g. straws, popsticks, marbles, scoops of rice). Say: Make a unit that is ten times larger to use to measure things in the room. Call this a deca-straw (deca-popstick, deca-marble, deca-scoop). Encourage them to use the language during measuring in multiples of 10 units. (e.g. *This tub takes 13 scoops; that means it takes 1 deca-scoop and 3 scoops*.)

Popstick Widths

Invite students to use a ruler to find something that is a centimetre wide (e.g. width of a popstick). Ask: How many go together to make a decimetre? Can you find something that is a decimetre wide? How many decimetres go together to make a metre? Help students find out how many popstick widths go together to make a metre.

Charts 1

Have students gather labels that show measurements and use them to create a chart for each attribute (mass, capacity, length). On their chart, have them order the labels from smallest to biggest. Ask: Are millilitres bigger or smaller than litres?

Charts 2

As students handle and explore units for mass, capacity and length, set up charts that show a gram, a litre and a metre. Add the *deci-* and *deca-*, the *centi-* and *hecto-*, and the *milli-* and *kilo-* prefixes over time. Have students draw pictures of objects that match each of the measures and add them to the chart. (Students are not expected to remember or learn these names; the purpose is to expose them to the consistencies in the system.)

KU 8

SAMPLE LEARNING ACTIVITIES

Middle ✔✔

Metres to Decimetres

Have groups of students make a metre-length tape and use it to measure how far they can jump. Draw out the limitations in the size of the unit and help students divide the metre into tenths. Name them as decimetres and ask students to use them to compare the distances.

Decimetres to Centimetres

Ask students to use decimetres to measure pencil lengths. Ask: What is the problem with decimetres? What could we do? Help students divide the decimetre into tenths. Ask: What is the name of this unit? How many are in a metre?

Deca-Jumps

Have students explore the relationship between the milli unit, the centi unit, the unit and the deca unit. For example, invite them to construct a measuring tape based on a familiar distance (e.g. their jump, their stride). First, have them cut a length of tape to show their deca-jump (deca-stride), which is ten times their jump (stride). Then, invite them to mark in the jump unit (stride unit), followed by their deci-jumps (deci-strides) and their centi-jumps (centi-strides). Ask: How would you mark in milli-jumps (milli-strides)? Encourage students to use their tapes for measuring.

Trundle Wheel

Ask groups of students to use string to measure the perimeter of a large round lid and give the unit a name (e.g. lids). Help them to make the lid into a trundle wheel and invite them to measure distances around the school by counting the units. When students have recorded their distances, ask them to record them using the name of the unit and the prefixes *deca-*, *hecto-* and *kilo-*. Ask: What could you call the unit for 10 lids? What could you call the unit for 100 lids? (e.g. lids, deca-lids, hecto-lids, kilo-lids) Draw out that 10 units will use the prefix *deca-* and 100 units will use the prefix *hecto-*. Help children to use their calculators to see that the unit gets ten times larger each time.

One Hundred Items

Ask students to use one hundred items (e.g. nails or beads in a pre-sealed plastic bag) as a unit to weigh things in the classroom (e.g. a pile of books). Invite them to give the unit a name (e.g. nails, beads). Ask: Is this unit useful to help work out how much one book weighs? Help students to divide the unit into ten small bags of ten which they name using the prefix *deci-* (e.g. deci-nails, deci-beads) and again into ten single nails, which they name using the prefix *centi-* (e.g. centi-nails, centi-beads). Ask: What do *deci-* and *centi-* mean? Why are they used in this way?

Grouping Cubes to Weigh

Following 'One Hundred Items', invite students to use loose linking centimetre cubes (with a weight of 1 gram each) with a balance scale to find the weight of objects. Ask: How can we group these to make counting easier? (in tens, in hundreds) What prefix could we use for the weight of 10 cubes (100 cubes)? (e.g. deca-cubes, hecto-cubes) After students have constructed decagram, hectogram and kilogram units, have them weigh the units, using kitchen scales to link the units to those on the dial. Ask: How many cubes did you need for a kilogram?

Medicine

Have students use measuring containers and water to solve the following problem. Say: I need to take 10 mL of medicine a day and I buy it in 100-mL bottles. How many days will it last? If I buy a 1-litre bottle, how long will it last? Ask: What information will help you work it out? What do you think the unit names for 10 mL (centilitre) and 100 mL (decilitre) would be? Refer to what they know about length measures and the use of the prefixes *centi-* and *deci-*. Encourage students to use a calculator to check their results.

Meaning of Prefixes

Have groups of students find words from dictionaries (computers, items around the room) that begin with the prefixes *milli-*, *centi-*, *deci-*, *deca-*, *hecto-* and *kilo-*. Encourage students to discuss what they mean and use words and diagrams to illustrate their meaning.

Units of Time

Have students create a chart to show the relationships between units of time (e.g. year, month, week, day, hour, minute). Ask: Why don't we use the prefixes *kilo-* and *centi-* when we talk about time? (Time is not metric, although we now use the metric prefixes *milli-*, *micro-*, and *nano-* to divide seconds into smaller units.)

KU 8

SAMPLE LEARNING ACTIVITIES

Later ✔✔✔

A Millimetre Thick

Invite students to use a ruler to find something that is a millimetre thick (e.g. a paper clip). Ask: How many do you need to put together to make a centimetre (decimetre, metre, decametre)? (Link to *First Steps in Mathematics: Number*, Understand Whole and Decimal Numbers, Key Understanding 8.)

Metric Prefixes

Have students collect and categorise the names of known standard units to explore relationships in metric measures. For example, after listing all the units students know, focus on metric units of length, mass and capacity. Invite students to sort the units from smallest to largest and match up words with the same prefixes before exploring the quantity relationships between units. Ask: How are kilometres and metres similar to kilograms and grams? (Both are 1000 times larger.) What does this tell you about kilolitres? (Must be equal to 1000 litres.) Have we missed any? Could there be a unit called 'centigram' or a 'centilitre'? (See Sample Lesson 4, page 84.)

Length	Mass	Capacity
millimetre	gram	millilitre
centimetre	kilogram	litre
metre		kilolitre
kilometre		

Design a Measurement System

Have students select a base unit for mass, volume and length (e.g. the amount of play dough that will fit in a small cubic box might give the base unit for volume and mass, and the height of the box could be the length unit). Invite groups of students to make up a name for each unit and develop larger and smaller units (deca-name, deci-name, centi-name). Ask: How do you know how many of your deci-units of length equals your deca-unit?

Displacement

Give groups of students measures with millilitre calibrations (e.g. medicine cups). Have them use displacement of water to find the volume of a rock (marble, washer) in millilitres. Ask them to work together to find how many centimetre cubes displace an equal amount of water. Draw out the observation that 1 cubic centimetre displaces 1 millilitre of water. (See Did You Know?, page 86.)

Mass, Volume and Capacity

Have students explore the relationships in the metric system between mass, volume and capacity. Invite pairs of students to weigh a 1-litre milk carton full of water and record its mass. Ask them to use displacement of water to find the volume in litres of a decimetre cube (1000 cubic centimetres) and record it. Ask: What does this show? Help them see that a litre equals 1000 cubic centimetres in volume, which equals a kilogram of water. Ask: What does this tell us about one cubic centimetre of water? Would you expect a decimetre cube of wood to weigh one kilogram? Why? Why not?

Sweets Problems

Have students work on problems such as the following. Say: Sweets are sold in bulk for £10 per kilogram. How much would it cost to buy 100 grams (10 grams)? Or, say: One-hundred-gram bags of prepacked sweets cost £1.65 each, and 1-kilogram bags cost £15. Which is the cheapest way to buy a kilogram of them? Encourage students to use their own methods to calculate the results, then compare strategies. Ask: Were some ways easier than others? Which strategy made it easier to work out? How do the x 10 value relationships help you calculate? (Link to *First Steps in Mathematics: Number*, Operate, Key Understandings 3 and 4, Calculate, Key Understanding 4.)

Sorting Cards

Extend Later Sample Learning Activity 'Sorting Cards' (Key Understanding 5) by asking questions as the students compare the two measures, such as: What is the relationship between the two units? How many times larger or smaller is one unit than the other? (See Key Understandings 3 and 5.)

Shadows

Have students use MAB flats or decimetre squares of paper to find the area of irregular shapes such as their shadows. Invite them to discuss and justify their strategies for ensuring all of the shape is included in their area measure. Ask: How can the decimetre square be subdivided to help you include all the shape? Would centimetre grid paper help? If you've found 215 square centimetres, how many decimetre squares is this? How do you know? (See Direct Measure, Key Understanding 5.)

KU 8

Later ✔✔✔

Length and Square Units

Have students explore the relationship between units of length and units of area. For example, invite them to draw a 1-centimetre line next to a 1-decimetre line on grid paper and, underneath, a 1-centimetre square next to a 1-decimetre square. Ask: How many 1-centimetre lengths fit along the 1-decimetre line? (ten) So, how many 1-centimetre squares *must* fit across the top of the 1-decimetre square (ten) and how many *rows* of ten 1-centimetre squares are needed to cover the 1-decimetre square? (ten) How many square centimetres altogether? (10 x 10, or 100) Draw out that the area of the decimetre square in square centimetres is equal to the centimetre length *squared*. Have students explore other length and area unit relationships to show how this is true for any length units. For example, 100 centimetres equals 1 metre, so 100 *squared* (100 x 100) tells you how many square centimetres in a square metre.

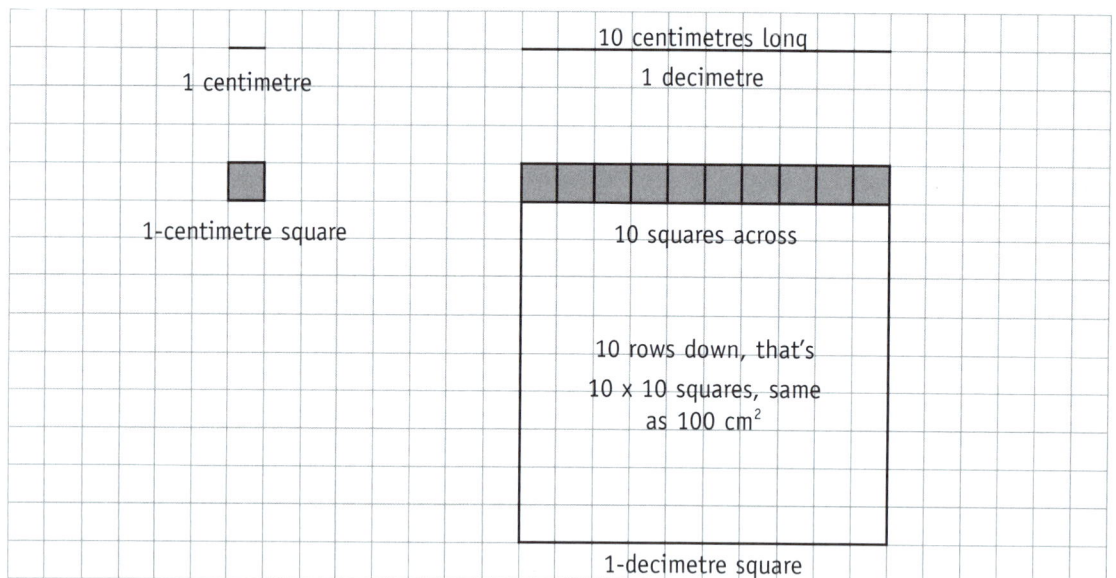

1 centimetre	10 centimetres long
	1 decimetre
1-centimetre square	10 squares across
	10 rows down, that's
	10 x 10 squares, same as 100 cm^2
	1-decimetre square

Length and Cubic Units

Extend 'Length and Square Units' by using MAB materials to show how length units relate to volume. For example, to show how many cubic centimetres are equal to a cubic decimetre, help students see that ten in a row by ten rows by ten layers (10 *cubed*) of 1-centimetre cubes builds a 1-decimetre cube. Draw out the idea that if 10 centimetres equals 1 decimetre, then 10 *cubed* must be the number of cubic centimetres in a cubic decimetre. Help students see the logical relationships between standard length units (one-dimensional units), standard area units (two-dimensional units) and standard volume units (three-dimensional units).

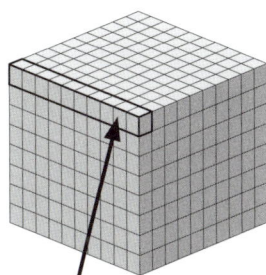

Ten 1-centimetre cubes fit across a 1-decimetre cube.

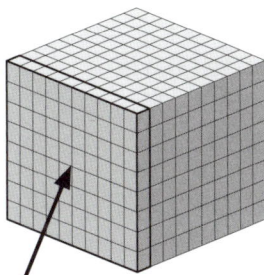

Ten rows of ten 1-centimetre cubes make one layer of 100 1-centimetre cubes.

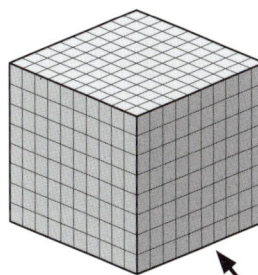

Ten layers of 100 1-centimetre cubes make one 1-decimetre cube made of 1000 1-centimetre cubes.

10 cm

|——— 10 cm ———|

1 dm = 10 cm

LENGTH

(one-dimensional unit)

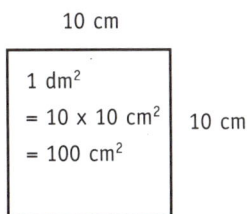

10 cm

1 dm^2
= 10 x 10 cm^2
= 100 cm^2

10 cm

AREA

(two-dimensional unit)

length *squared*

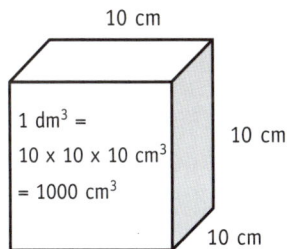

10 cm

1 dm^3 =
10 x 10 x 10 cm^3
= 1000 cm^3

10 cm

10 cm

VOLUME

(three-dimensional unit)

length *cubed*

KU 8

SAMPLE LESSON 4

Sample Learning Activity: Later—'Metric Prefixes', page 80

Key Understanding 8: The relationships between standard units in the metric system help us to judge size, move between units and do calculations.

Teacher's Purpose

I overheard two of my Year 7 boys talking about swimming practice for our swimming carnival.

'I swam a kilometre,' boasted David.

'How do you know?' asked Josh.

'Well, the swimming coach told me that the big pool is fifty metres, so I worked out that one lap, that's two lengths, that's two fifties—a hundred metres every lap, so ten laps ends up a thousand metres. That's a kilometre,' said David.

While I was quite impressed by his calculations, Josh was still doubtful. 'How do you know a thousand metres is a kilometre?' he asked.

I was expecting David to refer to the fact that *kilo* means 'thousand', but there was just a dismissive shrug, 'There is!' and the conversation ended there. This made me wonder whether there were others in the class who knew isolated measurement facts, such as a thousand metres equals a kilometre, but did not recognise the underpinning pattern and logic that made metric measures so easy to use.

Action and Reflection

We began by having small groups of students brainstorm the names (not symbols) of measurement units (e.g. kilograms, centimetres, litres, millimetres) and then sort the units firstly according to whether they were metric or not and then according to the attributes the units measured (i.e. mass, length, area and volume and capacity). The non-metric units were put aside for the remainder of this lesson, to be discussed at a later date. The metric units were then listed from smallest to largest for each attribute. When all had finished ordering their lists, we compared them as a class and came to a consensus about the names and the order of units for each attribute. I wanted the students to work from what they knew rather than what I knew, so I did not volunteer any names for units that were missing, nor question how they arrived at the order.

Because I did not want them to become distracted at this stage by the effects of squaring and cubing length units, I suggested we ignore the 'square' and 'cubic' measures for the moment and just focus on the three groups of basic unit words. We matched up parts of words so that we ended up with the following wall display:

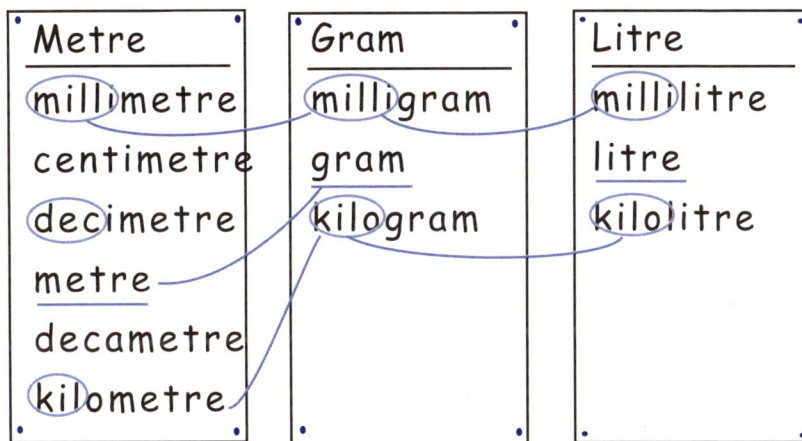

Students talked about what they saw:
'None of the lines cross over.'
'Metres have got lots more names.'
'Milli and kilo are in all the lists.'
'There's some leftovers—centi, deca, and deci are only in the metres.'

At that point, Carrie had her dictionary out. 'But you can have a decigram and a decilitre and a decalitre and a decagram; look they're all in here!'

I reminded students about other reference material around the classroom. Students began looking for 'centigram' and 'centilitre'. We added them to the gram and litre charts so that all of the metre prefixes had their equivalent mass and capacity units listed.

Connection and Challenge

Once the students thought they had derived all the unit names, I asked them to work out how many of each unit equalled the next-sized units. After studying their lists and dictionaries, it didn't take long for several in the class to excitedly exclaim, 'It's always ten!'

Kirsten shook her head, 'It's not *always* ten; a kilogram is 100 decagrams, not ten, and that goes for litres and metres as well.'

After other students checked to confirm this anomaly, a number of students suggested that there had to be a prefix for 'ten times deca'. At this point, I conceded that there was a prefix for it, though it was not commonly known, and suggested they look up *hecto* in their dictionaries. We then completed our charts and added the different values for each unit.

Some students researched the prefix naming system a little further and found there were names for even smaller units than 'milli-units' (e.g. 'micro-', 'nano-' and 'pico-units') and larger units than 'kilo-units' (e.g. 'mega-', 'giga-' and 'tera-units'), which made jumps of a thousand times the value between units rather than just ten times. We talked about Olympic race times and wondered what sorts of measuring situations would need accuracy to a picometre, which is one billionth of a millimetre!

KU 8

LENGTH	
millimetre	thousandth of a metre
centimetre	hundredth of a metre
decimetre	tenth of a metre
metre	ONE METRE
decametre	ten metres
hectometre	hundred metres
kilometre	thousand metres

MASS	
milligram	thousandth of a gram
centigram	hundredth of a gram
decigram	tenth of a gram
gram	ONE GRAM
decagram	ten grams
hectogram	hundred grams
kilogram	thousand grams

VOLUME/CAPACITY (LITRES)	
millilitre	thousandth of a litre
centilitre	hundredth of a litre
decilitre	tenth of a litre
litre	ONE LITRE
decalitre	ten litres
hectolitre	hundred litres
kilolitre	thousand litres

In the following days, we went on to match the various prefixes to decimal number place values and explored the ease with which we could make conversions based on this knowledge about these commonalities; for example:

1.243 km = 12.43 hectometre = 124.3 decametre = 1243 m = 12 430 dm = 124 300 cm = 1 243 000 mm

? Did You Know?

A link between some different attributes has been designed into the metric system:

1 kilogram is defined to be the mass of 1 litre of water

and   1 litre is defined to be the same volume as 1 cubic decimetre

hence   1 cubic decimetre of water has a mass of 1 kilogram

but   1 cubic centimetre is a thousandth of a cubic decimetre

so   1 cubic centimetre of water has a mass of one thousandth of a kilogram

so   1 cubic centimetre of water weighs 1 gram

But be careful—we can't assume it is true of other materials, which might be heavier or lighter.

CHAPTER 3

Direct Measure

Carry out measurements of length, capacity/volume, mass, area, time and angle to needed levels of accuracy.

This chapter will support teachers in developing teaching and learning plans that relate to this outcome:

Overall Description

Students use common measuring equipment and graduated scales such as rulers, clocks, kitchen scales and grids, choosing equipment or techniques to suit their situation. They understand the importance of making measurements accurately and consistently; for example, making sure the cup is always filled to the same level when measuring capacity, or adjusting for the weight of the container when weighing butter for a recipe. They express measurements in correct units and use their understanding of the common metric prefixes to move flexibly between units and to judge size. They make things using measurement specifications; for example, an open box to hold at least 1 litre of orange juice, or marking out the field for a game of softball or tee ball. They judge and measure time, using the various natural cycles in their environment, or available technologies, such as clocks and calendars. They know the difference between time and elapsed time and can calculate the amount of time between 2:05 a.m. and 1:45 p.m. in order to set the video recorder or to prepare and read timetables and programs.

Key Understandings

Teachers will need to plan learning experiences that include and develop the following Key Understandings (KU), which underpin achievement of the outcome. The learning experiences should connect to students' current knowledge and understandings rather than to their year level.

Key Understanding	Stage of Primary Schooling— Major Emphasis	KU Description	Sample Learning Activities
KU1 We can directly compare objects and events to say which has more length, mass, capacity, area, volume, angle or time.	Beginning ✔✔✔ Middle ✔✔ Later ✔	page 89	Beginning, page 91 Middle, page 94 Later, page 97
KU2 We can indirectly compare two objects by using other objects as go-betweens or by altering the objects in some way that doesn't affect the quantity.	Beginning ✔✔✔ Middle ✔✔ Later ✔✔	page 103	Beginning, page 105 Middle, page 107 Later, page 109
KU3 To measure consistently we need to use our instrument in a way that ensures a good match of the unit with the object to be measured.	Beginning ✔✔ Middle ✔✔✔ Later ✔✔✔	page 111	Beginning, page 113 Middle, page 115 Later, page 117
KU4 Calibrated scales can be used as a substitute for repeating units when measuring length, capacity, mass, angle and time.	Beginning ✔✔ Middle ✔✔✔ Later ✔✔✔	page 119	Beginning, page 121 Middle, page 123 Later, page 126
KU5 Units are quantities and so we can use different representations of the same unit so long as we do not change the quantity.	Beginning ✔ Middle ✔✔ Later ✔✔✔	page 133	Beginning, page 135 Middle, page 137 Later, page 139
KU6 We can judge and measure time using both natural cyclical changes and special techniques and tools which people have developed.	Beginning ✔ Middle ✔✔ Later ✔✔✔	page 145	Beginning, page 147 Middle, page 150 Later, page 153

Key

✔✔✔ The development of this Key Understanding is a major focus of planned activities.

✔✔ The development of this Key Understanding is an important focus of planned activities.

✔ Some activities may be planned to introduce this Key Understanding, to consolidate it, or to extend its application. The idea may also arise incidentally in conversations and routines that occur in the classroom.

KEY UNDERSTANDING 1

We can directly compare objects and events to say which has more length, mass, capacity, area, volume, angle or time.

A great deal can be learned about objects that we can see or hold, and events that are occurring, by directly comparing them. We stand one person next to another to see who is taller, place one pencil alongside another to see which is longer, pour from one container to another to see which holds more, heft two objects in our hands to judge which is heaviest, and place one sheet of paper over the other to see which has the greatest area. In obvious cases, we can even 'look' and see which object has the greatest volume. Sometimes a direct comparison is straightforward and it is relatively easy to reach a correct conclusion so long as we focus upon the right attribute. (See Understand Units, Key Understanding 1 for related experiences.) Often, however, it is neither completely straightforward nor obvious.

In order to make a direct comparison of length, the student must recognise the importance of ensuring that one end of each object is in the same position. With the heights of people, this is usually easy because we stand on the floor and the highest person is the tallest or longest. Were we to lie on the floor, the task would be different and more difficult since we would need to ensure that we matched the position of either our feet or our heads. Matching one end of each object is central in comparing lengths, but is a point that students often miss unless they are provided with learning experiences that draw their attention to it and help them make it explicit. Also, if we need to compare the lengths of curves, a direct comparison of length may be difficult or impossible and an indirect method needed (see Key Understanding 2).

Although the basic ideas underlying measurement are the same regardless of what is being measured, the actual process of comparison varies for different attributes, with some attributes being more difficult to compare than others. Students do not always draw the same conclusions as adults might from direct comparison, particularly with measures other than length. For example, students who appear to understand the functioning of a balance beam may allow the appearance of size to override the information provided by the balance and may also be distracted by the pointer and say that the thing on the side to which the pointer points is heaviest. Students who happily pour from one container to another may not recognise this as a way of showing which has more. In comparing the area of two shapes, students may try to do it by looking and not superimposing (sit one over the other) or making visual adjustments to balance non-overlapping parts. In comparing angles, they may find it difficult to focus upon the 'amount of turn' between the arms while ignoring the 'length' of the arms.

Students who are through the Matching and Comparing Phase can directly compare the length of straight things, lining up one end where necessary, and they use the comparison to say which are the same length, longer or shorter. They heft objects, one in each hand, to say which is heaviest where the difference in mass is easily discerned. They may, however, allow the appearance of size to influence their judgment.

As students move into the Quantifying Phase, they correctly interpret a balance beam and no longer allow the appearance of size to override the sense of weight. Asked to decide which of two regions has the greatest 'amount' (e.g. of pizza, of grass), they think of superimposing the regions as a strategy, although they may focus on some overlapping parts and ignore others. They will fully fill one container and carefully pour from that container to just fill a second in order to decide which container holds most.

Students who are through the Quantifying Phase will take more care to deal with all non-overlapping parts when superimposing to compare the area of two regions. They are able to directly compare two angles by the amount of turn and they understand that to directly compare how long two events take, generally each has to start (or finish) at the same time.

SAMPLE LEARNING ACTIVITIES

Beginning ✔✔✔

Trains

Vary Beginning Sample Learning Activity 'Trains' (Understand Units, Key Understanding 3) by having students line their trains up to compare the lengths. Ask them to make their trains the same length. Ask students to make two or more things that are the same length when they make snakes from play dough, or cut string or tape for collage and straws for beads. (See Key Understandings 2 and 3.)

Showing and Telling

When directly comparing quantities, model how you do it, and talk about what you do. For example, when comparing lengths, say: First I need to check that the lengths are lined up at the base, then I look at the tops. When comparing capacity, say: I need to make sure I fill my cup to the same level each time. When comparing mass, say: The one in this hand feels heavier, but I'll change hands and see if it still feels heavier in the other hand. When comparing area, say: I think I'll put them together to see which one hangs over the other one. For time, say: How will we know which takes longer if we both start at the same time? The one that finishes first is quicker.

Who Is Tallest?

Invite small groups of students to order themselves from shortest to tallest. Ask: If Quentin stood on this box, would he be the tallest? What about if he stood on his toes? What do we need to do to compare our height properly? Could we still find out who is the tallest if we all lie down? How? What would we need to do? (Link to Understand Units, Key Understanding 1.)

Imitative Play

During imitative play (e.g. in the sand pit, in the class shop), have students directly compare pieces of equipment ranging in size and number (e.g. chairs, cups, plates, bowls, spoons, blankets, bears, dolls, trucks, diggers, spades, buckets, trolleys). Ask: Which is taller? Which is wider? Which is heavier? How can you check?

Sorting Equipment

Have students sort equipment (e.g. balls, ropes, bean bags) by size. Discuss which attribute they are using to compare each type. Ask: What are you looking at to decide which one is bigger? Encourage them to describe how they decide which ones are the same size (longer, shorter, heavier, lighter, takes up more (less) space). Ask: How did you check them? (Link to Understand Units, Key Understanding 1.)

Using a Balance Scale

Extend Beginning Sample Learning Activity 'Using a Balance Scale' (Understand Units, Key Understanding 3) by asking: How can you make both sides of the scale be halfway up and halfway down? Encourage students to heft the objects to directly compare the mass and experience the fact that they are the same, then place them in the scales and watch the balance. Extend this to comparing objects with different mass and using other weighing tools. (See Sample Lesson 1, page 99.)

Pour to Decide

Give students two identical clear containers with one of them full of water. Focus students on the water and ask: If you pour the water into that container, will all of that water fit in or will there be some left over? After students have said what their ideas are, invite them to pour to decide. Ask: What happened? Do the containers hold the same amount of water? (See Understanding Units, Key Understandings 1 and 2.)

Pour to Decide Again

Extend 'Pour to Decide' by providing two different-sized clear containers. Stop the students pouring if the container is about to overflow and focus them on the water that is left in the first container. Ask: Is there too much water for this container? Does that container hold more water than this one? When students pour from the smaller container, ask: Could that container fit more in? Will that container hold more water? Which container holds the most water? Draw out the idea that the larger container holds more.

Jellies

Have students compare two jelly moulds or buckets similar in size. Ask: Can you tell just by looking which one holds the most? How could you check to be sure? Provide students with suitable materials (e.g. water, sand, rice) and invite them to try their strategies and consider the effect of filling one mould (bucket) and pouring into the other. Ask: Are there any leftovers? Do they hold the same amount? Does one hold more? Is there enough water (sand, rice)? (See Understand Units, Key Understanding 1.)

Beginning ✔✔✔

Cubes and Boxes

Extend the 'Jellies' activity by providing two boxes similar in size. Ask: Which box is bigger? Have students fill one box with cubes, then transfer the cubes to the second box. Ask: Are any blocks left over? Do you need more blocks to fill the second box? How does this help you say which box is bigger? Does it make a difference if you pack the cubes in the boxes very carefully?

Models

When making models of farms or towns, provide students with transparent shapes that do and do not match the areas of features in the models (e.g. parks, ponds, paddocks, sandpits). Have students compare the transparent shapes to the features and decide which are larger, smaller or the same size. Ask: How can you find out if this shape is bigger than the paddock (park, pond, sandpit)? Would putting it on top of the paddock help? (See Key Understanding 3.)

Ordering Containers

Give groups of students a range of different-sized containers. Ask: Will the tallest one hold the most? How are these two different? After students have handled the containers and ordered them by height, ask: What other ways could the containers be ordered?

Superimpose

During various classroom activities, find opportunities to have students superimpose to find areas (e.g. choose a cover for the computer keyboard, tablecloths for different tables, tangram shapes for pre-drawn pictures, place a foot against the undersole of a shoe, lids on jars).

SAMPLE LEARNING ACTIVITIES

Middle ✔✔

Sports Day

For sports day, cut faction ribbons into a number of different lengths and mix them together. Have students sort the ribbons by length and put them into different boxes. Ask: How can you be sure all the ribbons in each box are the same length?

Pizza Trays

Show students two pizza baking trays, one a rectangle and the other a circle. Say: The pizza shop charges the same price for both these pizzas. Is there more to eat in the rectangular pizza, or the circular pizza? How would you decide? Provide cut-out models of the trays and suggest students superimpose to decide. Ask: Do you think the bit around the edge of the rectangle will fit into the bit around the edge of the circle? (See Key Understanding 2 and Indirect Measure, Key Understanding 1.)

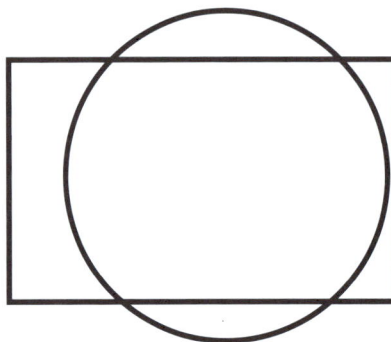

Smaller but Heavier

Ask students to think about this statement: You can't tell if one object is heavier than another just by looking. Ask: Is this correct? Provide balance scales and a variety of materials (e.g. fruit, vegetables, pencil cases, tissue boxes, tape dispenser, paperweight). Invite students to find objects that look small but weigh more than larger objects. Ask: What is it that makes this small object weigh more than the larger object? Which would weigh more if they were both made of the same material?

Looking at the Pointer

During mass activities such as 'Smaller but Heavier', ask: Is the pointer on the balance scales pointing to the side that has the heavy object? How is this different from when we just look at which side is going down? (Link to Key Understanding 3.)

Middle ✔✔

Have students use two pouches sewn to the end of two strips of elastic to compare the weight of objects. Ask: How is this different from using a balance scale? If both objects stretch the elastic downwards (instead of one going up and one going down) how can we tell which is heavier? Why is it important to hold the tops of both strips of elastic at the same height?

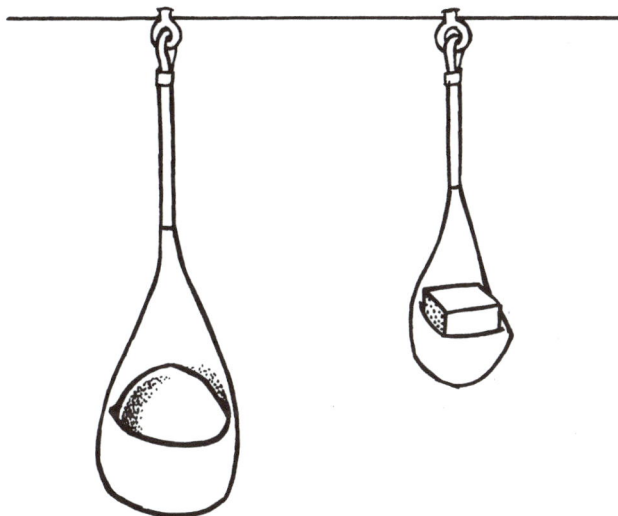

Capacity and Shape

Have students look at several containers that are close in capacity, but different in shape. Ask: Which container would hold the most water? What makes you think so? Invite them to check by pouring water from one to the other.

Fitting Boxes

Invite students to fit boxes inside other boxes in order to work out which has the largest volume. Ask: How can you tell which has more volume? What if a box does not fit because its shape is different? How can you find out which is bigger? How would thinking about 'which box holds more' help you to find a way to compare volume?

Groundsheet for a Picnic

Invite students to work out which of two big pieces of cloth would make the largest groundsheet for a picnic. Ask: What would be the best way of telling which is the largest? Suggest they put them together (superimpose) to try to judge. Ask: How can we tell which is larger when both have sections overlapping?

Comparing Time Taken

Have students discover the importance of using the same start time when directly comparing the time taken for various classroom activities (e.g. sharpening a pencil, putting on shoes, going for a drink of water, writing their name and date on the top of the page). Vary the start times when making comparisons and focus initially on who finishes first. Ask: Is this comparison fair? Why? Why not? How can we find out who really takes the least time? How can we make sure both begin putting on their shoes at the same time?

Book Corners

Have pairs of students use the corners of a book to find corners around the classroom with the same angle. Encourage them to draw each one and label it. Invite students to compare their angles to the corners of a square and introduce the language 'right angle' and '90 degrees' to describe the size of the angles. Then, ask students to find angles that are more or less than the right angle (90 degrees). Ask: Why do you think right angles are so common? What would happen if cereal packages were made with angles less than 90 degrees? How would they stack on the shelves?

SAMPLE LEARNING ACTIVITIES

Later ✔

Ordering Packages by Volume

Give groups of students a variety of packages (e.g. cereal cartons, tissue boxes, laundry detergent boxes). Ask them to directly compare and order them according to volume. Discuss their strategies. For example, ask: How did you decide which had more volume than another? What parts of the packages did you compare? Is it difficult to be sure that one package has greater volume than another? Why? Why not?

Who Is First?

Focus on directly comparing very short time intervals and the difficulties of ensuring identical starting points. For example, say: We are going to see who can sign their name the fastest (who is first to stand up from sitting cross-legged). How could we make sure that everyone starts at the same time? What would be a fair starting signal? How do we know when someone has finished? (Link to Key Understanding 6 and Understand Units, Key Understanding 1.)

Ordering Angles

Have students use a number of different 'angles' made from varying lengths of straws (pipe cleaners, bent wire) to order the size of some angles. Ask: When you decided which one was the largest angle, what did you compare? What made you put the angle made from the longest straws (pipe cleaners, bent wire) after the one made with the shortest straws (pipe cleaners, bent wire)? Show me two that have the same angle but are made from different length straws (pipe cleaners, wire). How do you know they have the same angle? (Link to Understand Units, Key Understanding 1.)

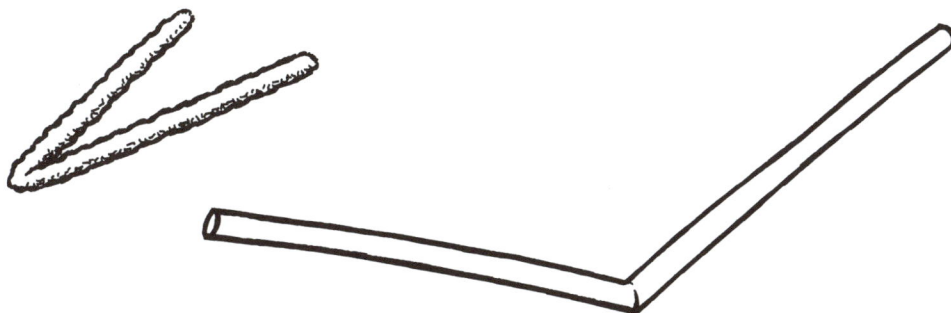

Washer in the Drink Carton

Have students use balance scales to directly compare the mass of nine sand-filled small drink cartons. To prepare for the following problem-solving puzzle, add a metal nut or washer to one of the cartons after balancing, then seal them all. Say: The manufacturer knows something fell into one of these nine cartons during packing, making it slightly heavier. You are to find out which carton has the extra mass, but you are only allowed to use the balance scales twice. (Answer: Compare a group of three with another group of three, to find which set of three has the extra, then take the heavier group and compare two of the cartons, to determine which it is. If the scales balance, the heavier carton cannot be on it, so the remaining carton must weigh more than the others.)

Olympic Sports

Have students sort situations into those where direct comparisons are made and those where direct comparisons cannot be made. For example, ask students to list those Olympic sports that are judged by direct comparison (those sports with identical starting times, such as swimming, so that whoever finishes first also takes the least time) and those that are not. Ask: In which sports are all the contestants on the field at once? Can the winning places of these sports all be judged using direct comparison? Why? Why not?

SAMPLE LESSON 1

Sample Learning Activity: Beginning—'Using a Balance Scale', page 92

Key Understanding 1: We can directly compare objects and events to say which has more length, mass, capacity, area, volume, angle or time.

Teacher's Purpose

I noticed that some of my pre-primary students seemed to have difficulty using the balance scales. Chelsea held down one side containing objects and filled the other side to overflowing, then let go. As the side she held rose, she pushed it back down and tried to make it stay down. She announced, 'They didn't work!' and became uninterested in using them.

Later, I gathered the class together. I wanted to teach them to handle the scales properly and to hear one another's ideas as they did so. I asked Chelsea why she thought the scales didn't work.

'When you put things in, both of the sides don't stay down. It keeps coming up.'

'Yeah,' said James, 'I push really hard and it won't go down.'

Terry nodded.

I drew their attention to the fact that the empty tubs were level and asked them what happened when one side of the scales was pushed down. 'How do the tubs move? Do they always do that?'

Chelsea didn't respond.

Their replies made me realise they had been focused on the task, but expected the scales to respond the same way their hands did when hefting; that is, both sides go down if they 'feel' heavy.

Connection and Challenge

I asked James to cup both hands, placed a rock in one of them and asked, 'Do your hands feel different, James?'

He shook the hand with the rock in it and said, 'This one's heavy.'

I asked the class to think what would happen if James put the rock in one side of the scales. Many said, 'It will go down!'

The students were buoyed by the result when James tried it. 'Why did the side with the rock in it go down?' I asked.

Terry replied, 'Because it's got something in it.'

I had wanted him to say 'because it was heavy'. I was getting ready to ask, 'Why did the rock make your hand go down?' when Phillipe said, 'That one goes down because it's heavier and that one will stay up because it's lighter. The heavy one always goes down. I'll show you.'

Phillipe chose a larger block and put it in the empty side. The larger block was actually lighter than the small rock and so it stayed up.

He was shocked by this. 'The block should be heavier than the rock! That's funny!'

He regained his composure and went on. 'Well, heavy things should make the side go down. Well, you see ... well, if that one's lighter, it goes up.'

He was unable to explain his thoughts. He had seen something that was in direct conflict with his firm belief that larger objects are heavier.

I took both objects out and said, 'Let's check. Which one is lighter?'

I gave them to Phillipe to help him see that the scales were right. Then I passed them to James. He hefted with both hands and said, 'The rock is heavy.'

I asked him to place the light object in one side of the scales, then the heavy one in the other and asked Terry to say what had happened. 'The rock one's gone down!'

I asked Chelsea, 'Did that surprise you?'

She responded, 'The block should go down, too.'

Action and Reflection

I asked everyone to choose two items from a collection of smallish items, to hold an item in each hand and decide which one was heavier. I then asked them to think about what the scales would do when they put the things in. I wasn't sure whether Amy knew about using the scales and so I asked, 'What will the scales do if you put your marble on one side and your lid in the other?'

She shrugged and said, 'The marble side will go down?'

I asked Terry, James and Chelsea to heft Amy's objects and say if they all agreed that her marble was heavier. I asked everyone to decide which side would go down, the side with the lid or the side with the marble. As we watched, Amy placed the items in the tubs. I asked Rachel to repeat this using Amy's two items, but changing the sides each time. After each turn I asked:

Later in that day, I gathered the five students who, like Phillipe, were convinced that larger must be heavier around the scales to compare large light objects with small, heavier objects.

'Which object did Amy say was heavier?'

'Which side is it in?'

'What did that side do?'

'What did the side with the lighter object do?'

After several turns, I asked, 'Did the light thing ever go down instead of the heavy thing?'

They all agreed that the heavy thing went down each time. I noticed in particular that Terry, James and Chelsea all nodded. I then asked, 'Why?'

James said, 'This one makes that one stay up.'

When I asked why it did that, he said, 'Because it's heavy.'

Practising with the New Ideas

One of the groups that I later gathered around the scales was Terry, James, Chelsea and Amy, to repeat the hefting to compare and notice the positioning of the scales when comparing the objects they hefted. I gave them each two new objects and asked them to use the scales to find out which one was heavier. They could check what the scales told them by hefting afterwards.

I listened to their ideas as they talked together about what would happen and was relieved to know they had begun to predict which side would stay up and which would go down. They had moved on from expecting both sides to go down and stay down if they had something in them, to expecting the heavier side to go down.

> *A week after this lesson, I focused this group on the idea that the scales would balance if the weight of the objects were the same using a small object and play dough.*
>
> *When James noticed the scales level, he said, 'Look! They're weighing!'*

Did You Know?

The 'logic' of pouring from one container to another to see which holds more seems obvious to most adults. When young students pour, however, some become so focused on the container they are pouring from that they hardly notice what is happening to the other container. Only when the first container is empty, do they shift their focus to the second. If the second container is the smaller, it will now be full, but the students may not realise the significance of the water that overflowed. Thus, the comparison of the capacity of two containers by pouring from one to the other is not obvious to students and experience in pouring from one container to another may be insufficient for the mathematical learning to occur. We need to help students focus on what is happening to the water level in each container and how that relates to the relative capacity of the two containers.

KEY UNDERSTANDING 2

We can indirectly compare two objects by using other objects as go-betweens or by altering the objects in some way that doesn't affect the quantity.

Often, when a direct comparison of a particular attribute of two objects cannot easily be made, it is possible to indirectly compare them by the use of intermediaries. In essence, the indirect comparison of two objects involves finding or producing alternative objects that can be directly compared. The alternative objects are different from the originals, but share the *relevant quantities* with the originals.

For example, in order to compare the length of two curving paths, we could fit string along the curves, cut and straighten each piece of string, directly compare them and make an inference about the curved paths. The two pieces of string act as go-betweens. This is not an obvious process to young students. In order to make sense of it, they have to believe that:

- each piece of string is the same length as the curved paths it was fitted along

- straightening the string does not change its length

- lining up one end of the two strings does not change their lengths (see Key Understanding 1)

- the longer string must come from the longer path.

To compare the width of a door with the width of the furniture we want to slide through it, we could cut one piece of string to fit the width of the furniture and compare the string with the door width. This requires that students realise that if the string is less than the door width the furniture will slide through, but if the string is more than the door width the furniture will not slide through. This transitive thinking must be developed through and drawn from carefully structured activities.

To compare the areas of two differently shaped pieces of paper, we could alter the paper in a way that leaves the relevant quantity, area, unchanged. We might, for example, cut one piece and rearrange the bits and place them over the other piece. In effect, the altered shape acts as a go-between; it is different from the original in shape, and possibly in perimeter, but has the same area. To compare the volumes of two rocks, we might put each into separate identical containers of water and compare the change in the height of water.

When we use units to compare quantities, we are using the object that represents the unit as a go-between. Each of the above indirect comparison situations could have been dealt with by using an appropriate unit-based strategy (see Understand Units). For example, a tape measure could be used as a go-between to measure the girth of two trees, enabling an indirect comparison to be made. Rulers, tape measures, measuring cylinders and squared paper are obvious instruments of indirect comparison.

Students who are through the Matching Phase can indirectly compare lengths such as curved paths. Students moving into the Quantifying Phase can also indirectly compare capacities. While they will superimpose regions to compare areas, they are unlikely to have a reliable indirect strategy for dealing with non-overlapping parts.

Students who are through the Quantifying Phase, unprompted, will attempt to alter one or both of the regions to enable a direct comparison of area. They may, for example, cut and rearrange the pieces of one to fit it over the other. They will also, unprompted, elect to use a unit to make a numerical measurement to compare several things. They may, for example, count how many spoonfuls of rice each takes to fill.

Note: 'Indirect comparison' is not the same as 'indirect measurement'. Indirect comparison involves comparing two different objects using something as a go-between (the go-between may even be a ruler or measuring cylinder). Indirect measurement involves the calculation of one measurement from other related measurements.

SAMPLE LEARNING ACTIVITIES

Beginning ✔✔✔

Body Parts

Have students use a go-between to measure how far it is around various body parts. For example, invite students to use paper tape to measure around their heads (wrists). Ask: How do you know whose head (wrist) is biggest?

Trains

Vary Beginning Sample Learning Activity 'Trains' (Understand Units, Key Understanding 3) by asking students to cut a length of string to match the length of their train. Ask: How many carriages long is your train? If you make a train tomorrow, will it be longer or shorter than this one? How many blocks will you use to make it? Then, on the next day, have students make a new train and use the string to see if it is shorter or longer than their first train. Ask: How much longer or shorter is your train than yesterday? (See Key Understandings 1 and 3.)

Matching Fruit

Ask students to find an object that matches the mass of an apple (orange, banana). The next day, ask them to use the object to find a piece of fruit that matches the weight of yesterday's apple (orange, banana), one that is heavier and one that is lighter. Ask: How did you know the fruit weighed the same?

Pet Rock

Have students solve mass problems where direct comparison is not possible. For example, say: I have a pet rock at home that fits in a closed hand and weighs the same as eight marbles. Do any of you have a pet rock you think weighs more (less)? It has to be small enough to fit in a closed hand. Provide students with rocks of different weights and sizes and ask them to use marbles and balance scales to see if they can find a rock that weighs more (less) than the one at home. (Link to Understand Units, Key Understanding 3.)

Pouring and Scooping

Have students use different-sized containers to pour liquids and grains from one to another during play and food preparation. Focus students on both how much a container will hold as well as how much liquid, rice or sand there is to be held. Ask: Will this container hold all of the drink? How many scoops of sand will your truck hold?

Equal Shares

Have students decide how to make sure each person gets the same amount of water poured from a jug when each student has a different-sized, clear plastic cup. Try out each suggestion for students to say if they think they have as much as the others or if one has more. Extend the activity over two or three days for the students to think about and try many suggestions. Make a list of those suggestions that could and probably wouldn't make equal shares. Encourage students to use one cup as the go-between.

Stamps

Ask students to trace 10-centimetre-square areas on an A3 sheet of paper and cover one of the areas with a print using a chosen object as a stamp. Ask: Did your stamp cover the area without leaving gaps? Try another one of your areas to see if you can fit more stamps on. Did your stamps overlap to fit that many on? Try to fit as many stamps on the page as you can without overlapping. Try a different stamp to see how many you can fit with no gaps or overlaps. Which stamps will fit the most prints on without overlaps? Why?

SAMPLE LEARNING ACTIVITIES

Middle ✔✔

Oil Spills

Give pairs of students an A3 copy of a map showing two different oil spills. Ask them to compare the areas of the oil spills. Ask: Would it help to cut off the overlapping bit? Does it change the measurement if we cut up the oil spills?

Oil Spills Again

Extend 'Oil Spills' by asking students to use paper tiles to compare the spills. Ask: How can you fit the squares around the edges and into the gaps? Would cutting them up help?

Measuring Drink Containers

Present students with different-shaped drink containers filled with water and an empty, larger-capacity, narrow container. Invite students to take turns pouring the contents into the larger container, marking each level with coloured elastic bands, then pouring the water back again. Ask: How does this show which containers hold more than others? Is this a more useful way of ordering several containers than just pouring from one drink container to another? Why? Why not?

Circumference of Trees

Invite students to find a way to check whether the circumferences of trees in the playground are more or less than the length of the metre rule. Ask: What makes it difficult to use the metre rule itself? What else might you use? Encourage groups of students to make the comparisons, using a method they choose. Discuss the results. Ask: How can you be sure your method works? What would you say to convince someone that the circumference of that tree is more than the length of the metre rule? How is the object you used similar to the metre ruler? (Link to Understand Units, Key Understanding 4.)

Timing Basketball Goals

Have students suggest and try out strategies for comparing the time taken for activities that can't be carried out simultaneously. For example, say: If we didn't have a clock available, how could we decide who takes the least time to throw five basketball goals when we can only use one goal ring? Discuss the reliability of various methods (e.g. counting hand claps, using a sand timer, using a water clock, measuring the sun's shadow, measuring the distance a student walks).

Breakfast Cereal

Have students use a go-between to compare capacity. For example, give students a container each. Say: I have a container at home that holds ten cups of breakfast cereal. Will your container hold more or less than mine? Ask: What could you use to work it out? Does it matter if you don't have any breakfast cereal? (Link to Understand Units, Key Understanding 4.)

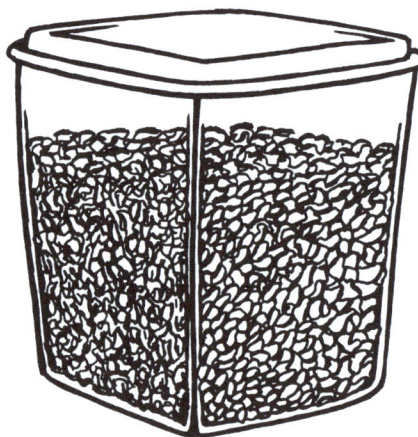

Sharing Play Dough

Ask groups of students to use balance scales to share a lump of play dough evenly between three people. Ask: Would using a go-between be helpful? (e.g. make each ball of play dough weigh the same as a tennis ball) Does the go-between need to be heavier or lighter? Later, extend the activity by asking: Would using units such as marbles, washers or gram weights be helpful? (Link to Understand Units, Key Understanding 6.)

Pizza Trays

Extend Middle Sample Learning Activity 'Pizza Trays' (Key Understanding 1), by asking: Can you cut and rearrange one of the shapes to find out which one is larger?

SAMPLE LEARNING ACTIVITIES

Later ✔✔

Paper Planes

Have students investigate ways to compare the distances paper planes will travel in a competition. Encourage them to discuss the aspects of distance involved and the difficulties in making comparisons. For example, ask: Should how far it goes up and down count? How can we measure it? What if it travels in a curved path? Give groups of students their choice of materials to make the paper planes and to compare distances during some trial flights. Decide as a class how to define 'distance travelled' for the competition and how the distances travelled will be compared. (Link to Understand Units, Key Understandings 5 and 6.)

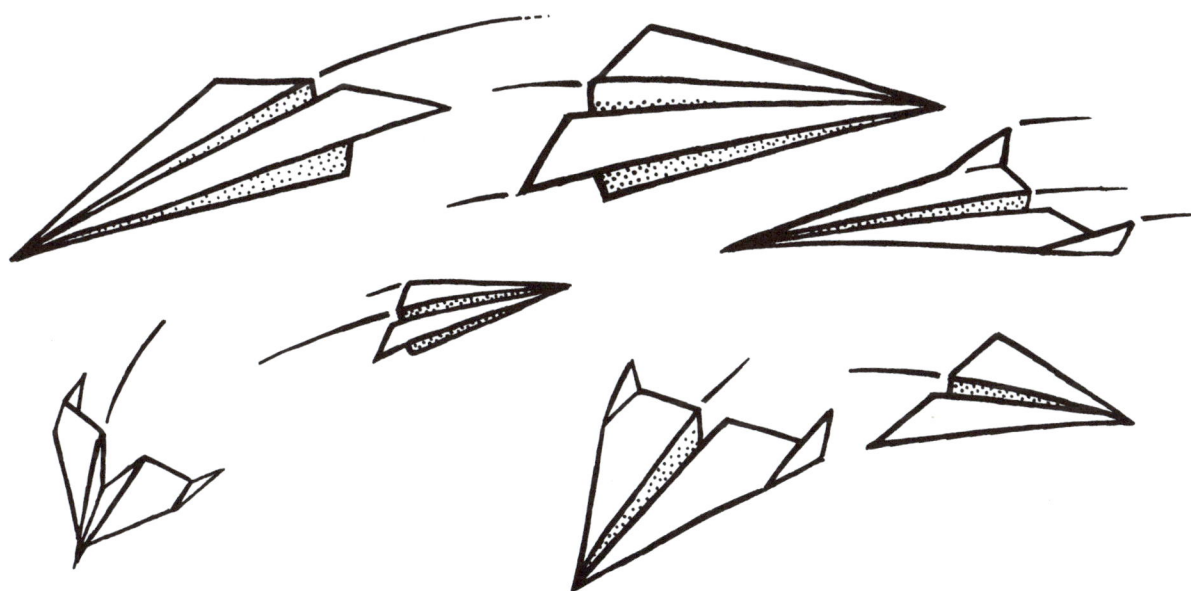

Surface Area

Have groups of students use their own strategies to compare the surface area of two sweets packets without cutting them up. Encourage students to discuss their strategies and their results. Ask: Which sweets packet uses more cardboard? How did you work it out? What did you use? Why? Would you have done it differently if I'd asked how much more cardboard was used? (Link to Understand Units, Key Understandings 3 and 6.)

Similar Solid Objects

Present students with two similar solid objects (e.g. small metal toys, china ornaments, drinking mugs). Ask: Which object has the greater volume? That is, which uses more material in its construction? Have students place the objects in a narrow container of water and watch what happens to the water level. Invite students to explore ways of marking or recording the levels to compare the volume of water displaced by each of the objects. Ask: What does the higher water level tell you about the amount of material used to make the objects? What would the displaced water be equal to if the object is hollow and the water doesn't get inside?

Grazing Areas

Say: There are two goats. The first goat is tethered by a lead to a stake in the ground. The second goat is tethered by a lead half as long as the first goat's lead to a sliding rail that is double the length of the first goat's lead. Invite students to use a compass and ruler to draw representations of the two feed areas. Ask: How would you work out which animal has access to the larger area? Encourage students to discuss and justify the method they chose. Ask: How could you convince someone that your method shows which animal has the larger feed area? (Link to Indirect Measure, Key Understanding 1, Understand Units, Key Understandings 4 and 6, and Direct Measure, Key Understanding 3.)

goat 1

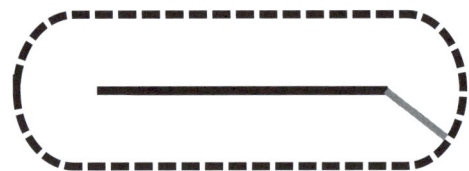

goat 2

KEY UNDERSTANDING 3

To measure consistently we need to use our instrument in a way that ensures a good match of the unit with the object to be measured.

To be able to think of 'counting units' as giving a description of the size of an object, we have to believe that if we measure the object a number of times with the same unit we should get the same result each time. This requires that we match the object to be measured with as many units as possible, but no more. Our capacity to do this reliably depends upon how well we choose measuring instruments to represent our unit and how carefully we use them. Key Understanding 4 in Understand Units emphasises choosing appropriate instruments to represent the unit, whereas this Key Understanding emphasises the practical skill of using them well. This Key Understanding, then, is about the skilful use of our measuring instrument, whether it is a pen repeated end-to-end or a trundle wheel, a plastic tile or a centimetre-square grid, a cup or a balance beam. The use of calibrated scales as described in Key Understanding 4 is one way of 'repeating units' and is therefore closely related to this Key Understanding.

Over time, students should come to see that in order to get reliable results they need to ensure that the unit size remains constant throughout and that they fit in as many as possible, but no more. This requires that they take care in several ways. Firstly, they need to ensure that the size of the things used as units remains uniform throughout the measuring process, checking:

- that the cup is always filled to the same level (capacity)
- that the beans are the same size (mass)
- that the tape measure isn't stretched in some places (length)
- that the ruler isn't broken on the end (length).

Secondly, they must use the 'unit' in a way that enables a good match with the object being measured, by:

- butting popsticks end-to-end (length) and not letting their fingers get in the way

- shaking their container to ensure there are no air pockets (capacity and volume)
- fitting shapes together with no gaps or overlaps (area and volume).

Thirdly, to ensure that the object is fully matched, but no more, they:

- place a book on their head and line up the book with the ruler (height)
- completely fill, but don't overfill, the container being measured (capacity)
- adjust for the container when weighing jelly beans (mass)
- fill as close as possible to the edge when covering regions (area).

Students who are through the Matching and Comparing Phase count informal units of capacity, mass and time. As suggested in Understand Units, however, they are likely to see the task literally as a counting task to see how many spoonfuls they happen to fit into the container or how many times they happen to have clapped while the music played. Because of this, students at this level may be casual in their use of instruments; for example, they may not really understand why it matters if they spill part of their spoonfuls.

As students move into the Quantifying Phase they begin to understand why it matters if they spill part of their spoonfuls and will repeat uniform units of length and capacity carefully, although they may still not understand what this has to do with, for example, lining up the zero on a ruler.

Students who are through the Quantifying Phase use uniform units consistently and carefully to measure quantities that are uni-dimensional, such as length, capacity and mass, as well as angle and time. They also use uniform units of area, although they may struggle with what to do along the edges when covering regions (see Key Understanding 5). While they may try to use some part-units of area, they may not be successful when it requires them to combine part-units.

Students who are through the Measuring Phase are able to use and combine part-units of area and hence can count units and part-units to find the area of any region. They can also count units of volume in straightforward cases.

Students who are through the Relating Phase, use a wide range of everyday instruments correctly.

SAMPLE LEARNING ACTIVITIES

Beginning ✔✔

Trains

Vary Beginning Sample Learning Activity 'Trains' (Understand Units, Key Understanding 3) by helping students notice when two trains with the same number of matching blocks are different lengths. Say: Look at the trains and see if you can work out why this train looks longer. Encourage students to make sure all of the blocks butt end-to-end. (See Key Understandings 1 and 2.)

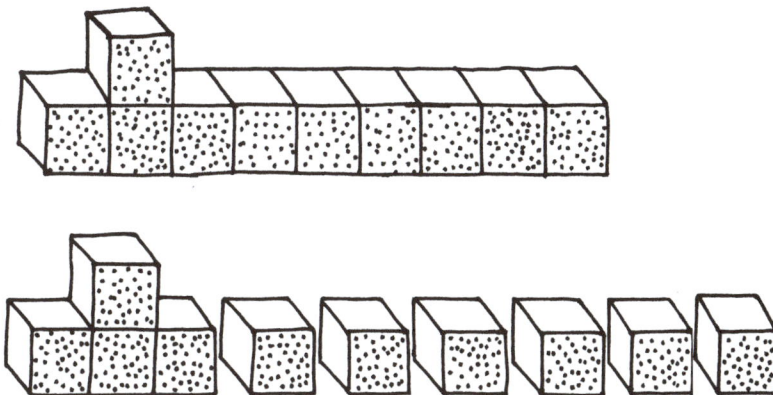

Packing Boxes

Have students pack blocks and other classroom equipment or materials into boxes, trying to fit in as many objects as they can. Ask: Could you fit more in? How could you pack it again so that there are not so many gaps? What makes a good fit? Why are the blocks easier to pack than the toy cars?

Paper Clips

Provide each student with one paper clip and ask them each to make a line five paper clips long. Display and compare the lines. Ask: Should the lines be the same length or different? Ask a student who has repeated the unit correctly, perhaps using a mark to show where to begin the next unit, to demonstrate how they made their line. Focus on the units butting end-to-end with no gaps or overlaps. Then, ask students to all make a new line twelve paper clips long and compare them again. Invite students to thread five paper clips together and match it to the first line. Ask: Why is the first line longer? Think about how we joined the clips.

Six-Cup Containers

Provide groups of students with containers that hold six to ten cups. Have students take turns measuring and recording how many cupfuls of water each container holds. Invite them to compare their results. Ask: Why might some of you have found that the same container holds a different amount of water? Encourage students to check their results two or three times. Ask: What are you doing to make the number of cupfuls more (less) than they should be? (e.g. spilling some, splashing more in, miscounting the cupfuls)

How Heavy Are Four Pieces of Fruit?

In small groups, have students measure how heavy four pieces of fruit are. Invite them to use the balance scales and a unit of their choice from paper clips, cubes, marbles, string, washers, sand and small cups. Ask students to explain why they chose their units and then compare their measurements with others. Ask: Why shouldn't we use different things as units?

Throwing

Vary Beginning Sample Learning Activity 'Furthest Throw' (Understand Units, Key Understandings 4 and 6) by having pairs of students work together to measure one throw. Invite one student to measure with their chosen unit, then have the other re-measure using the same unit. Ask: Why might you get different measures? What do you have to do to make sure your measures are both correct? (Link to Understand Units, Key Understandings 4 and 6, and Estimate, Key Understanding 1.)

SAMPLE LEARNING ACTIVITIES

Middle ✔✔✔

Length of a Desk

Ask students to use their pencils to measure and record the length of their desk. Ask: Are the results the same? Why? Why not? Invite students to demonstrate the way they used their pencil to obtain the measurements and to compare the lengths of their pencils. Ask: How would the length of your pencil make a difference? Did the way you measured affect your result? (Link to Understand Units, Key Understanding 4.)

Play Dough Balls and Mass

Give groups of students play dough and balance scales. Ask them to make small balls out of play dough to use as units for measuring and recording the mass of their toys (books, containers). Ask: Have you checked that the balance scales are level before you begin? How can you be sure each ball weighs exactly the same? Does it matter if they are not exactly the same? Does the pointer on the scales point to the light side or the heavy side? What makes you certain that eight of Carrie's balls will also balance your toy truck?

Play Dough Balls and Capacity

Extend 'Play Dough Balls and Mass' by having students use the same balls to measure the capacity of a range of containers. Ask: What happens if you squash the balls in for some and not for others? Would that give you a different measure? Why? Why not? (See Key Understanding 5; link to Understand Units, Key Understanding 4.)

Juice for an Excursion

Having decided in advance how many cups of juice are needed for an excursion, have students measure a set of containers to work out which will hold the right amount. Ask: If you don't completely fill each cup as you count, will we have a container that is too small or too big? If you spill a little each time, will that mean that you have counted more or less than you thought? (Link to Understand Units, Key Understanding 4.)

Spoonfuls of Flour

Have students compare their measurements with others to check for consistency. For example, say: The recipe for pancakes said to put in ten spoons of flour. Ask groups of students to measure out ten spoons of flour in identical, clear containers. Shake the flour level and display the containers in a row. Ask: Is there the same amount of flour in each container? Why? Why not? Compare two students' measures of ten spoonfuls and ask: Why are they different? Ask both students to measure again. Ask: What is different about the spoonfuls?

Recipe Measurements

Provide some recipe books and ask students to find out the size of common measurements used in recipes (e.g. tablespoons, teaspoons, cups). Ask: How can you make sure that each tablespoonful is the right size? As an experiment, have students make one cake where some of the measurements are either too small or too big and compare the results with another made with the exact measurements. Ask: Why do recipe books give information about the measures they use? (Link to Understand Units, Key Understanding 4.)

Area of Identical Shapes

Have groups of students use pattern blocks to measure the area of identical shapes. Invite them to compare the results and the arrangements used. Ask: Does it matter if you have used a different number of blocks? How do the different-shaped blocks affect the area? How can you compare area using different-shaped blocks? Have students suggest measuring 'rules' that would enable them to prove the shapes were all the same area; for example, say: Everyone use the same type of pattern block. Don't overlap the edges. Have students test the rules by measuring again and comparing results. Add more rules if necessary and practise applying the rules for other area comparisons. (Link to Understanding Units, Key Understanding 4.)

Oil Spills

Extend Middle Sample Learning Activity 'Oil Spills' (Key Understanding 2) by asking: Could you fit any more paper tiles onto the shape if you changed the way you have put them on? Do you have any paper tiles hanging over the edges? Are your squares all the same size? (Link to Understand Units, Key Understanding 4.)

Using Grid Paper

After area activities using repeated units (such as 'Oil Spills'), ask: Would grid paper help? Have students superimpose the shape onto the grid paper. Ask: How is this similar to gluing paper tiles onto the shape?

Faster Runner?

Say: By counting handclaps, Jason and Semina measured how long it took each other to run around the building. Semina claimed to be a faster runner because she took 34 claps, while Jason took 40 claps. Is Semina right?

SAMPLE LEARNING ACTIVITIES

Later ✔✔✔

Postage

Have students see that the instrument representing the unit must be of a consistent size when measuring. For example, say: Postage in a pretend country is worked out according to how many dried beans it takes to balance the envelope or package that is being sent. Invite groups of students to set up post offices and use the beans to test the mass of sets of postal items (identical for each group). Discuss the reasons for the variation. Ask: Why do some groups end up with a different mass? What problems might there be in using beans? Why might it be unfair to use beans to measure the mass of postal items? What could the Minister for Post Offices do to make sure that all post offices charge the same amount for identical items?

Garden Plots

Ask students to compare two different-shaped garden plots, one a rectangle (11 centimetres by 12 centimetres) and the other a right-angled triangle (17 centimetres by 15 centimetres). Give them a range of things to choose from to use as their unit, including matchsticks, 1-centimetre cubes, 2-centimetre cubes, pattern blocks, rice, counters and string. After they have completed their measurements, have students who have used the same units compare their results. Ask them then to share their work samples and strategies with the class. Ask: Were your measures different? Why? For example, ask students who used 1-centimetre cubes: Were you able to measure all of the shape with the 1-centimetre cubes? What did you do with the leftover bits? Ask groups using the same unit to repeat the measuring process, making sure they match as many units as possible, but no more, until they get the same result. (See Sample Lesson 2, Understand Units, page 35.)

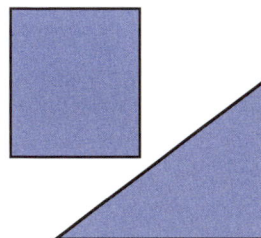

Gaps and Overlaps

Extend the 'Garden Plots' activity by asking: If you have gaps between your objects, have you overestimated or underestimated the size of the garden? How do you know? If you have overlapped your objects (or the edge), have you overestimated or underestimated the size of the garden? How do you know? Invite students to look at each other's work. In each case, ask: Has the size of the garden been overestimated? Why? Has it been underestimated? Why?

Fruit and Vegetables

Invite groups of students to choose one item of fruit or vegetable and agree on a unit to use to measure the surface area. Have students peel the item, spread the peelings as close together as possible on a plain sheet of paper and trace around them. Ask them to make a copy for each member of the group. Have students use their unit (e.g. centimetre grids, dotted grid paper, centimetre squared paper, tiles, cubes) to measure the area, then compare measures within the group. Ask: Were all the results the same? Why? What did you do with the bits that were outside the square? Repeat the measuring in order to get a more accurate measure. Have the group with the smallest range in their measures share their strategies. (See Understand Units, Key Understanding 4.)

Gaps and Overlaps

Extend 'Fruit and Vegetables' by examining work samples where there are gaps between the shape and the unit. Ask: Would this measure be an underestimate or an overestimate of the measure? Examine work samples where the unit overlaps the edge of the shape. Ask: Would these measures be an underestimate or an overestimate of the measure?

Treasure Hunt

Have students examine their measurement techniques in order to explain errors. For example, ask pairs of students to decide on the units and the appropriate instruments to design a treasure hunt around the school and then write distance and angle measurement instructions for another pair to follow to find the treasure. If the treasure is not easily found, decide if it was an error in the length or the angle measurement. Ask: How would you know which one caused the problem? For example, did you start and stop at the right spot with the trundle wheel? Did you use the correct angle of turn when changing direction? (See Understand Units, Key Understandings 3 and 6; link to Understand Units, Key Understanding 5.)

KEY UNDERSTANDING 4

Calibrated scales can be used as a substitute for repeating units when measuring length, capacity, mass, angle and time.

This Key Understanding is about the understanding and skill needed to use graduated scales (e.g. rulers, measuring jugs, kitchen scales, protractors, analogue clocks). This needs careful attention during the primary years. Students who are able to place centimetre blocks along a pencil and count 'how many', may not be able to use even a simplified ruler marked in centimetres. Also, some students, who can apparently use a simplified ruler may do so by rote and not connect it at all with the process of using centimetre blocks to measure. A child who 'forgets' to line up the beginning of an object to be measured with the zero mark on the ruler may well not understand the connection between measuring by repeating units and using a ruler.

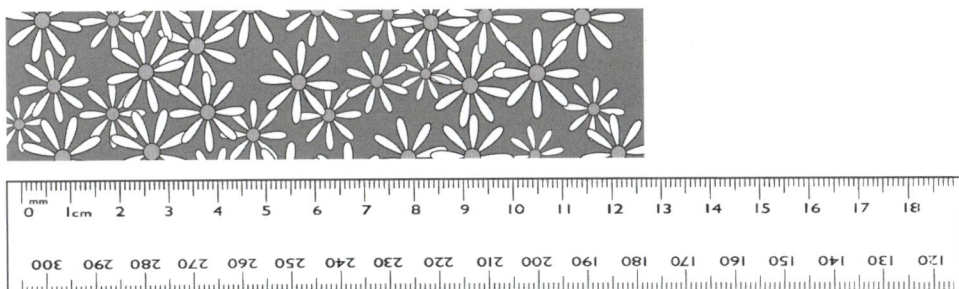

Simply reminding the student to 'line up the zero' does not deal with the basic conceptual problem. In essence, what the student is doing is failing to repeat the unit 'without gaps'; in 'matching' the object with the units marked on the ruler, the student has left an 'unmeasured' gap at the beginning of the object.

To link a conventional ruler with units of length, students need first to move from using multiple copies of a unit of length (perhaps a rod) to work out 'how many fit' to the idea that you can use one copy of the rod and 'mark it off' along the thing to be measured. From this, they should progress to making a tape measure using a unit such as the rod. They have to decide where the starting point is and realise why it is important to give it a label and why we label the ends of the units rather than the middle.

This:

and not this:

Students need to understand that the starting point shows the beginning of the first unit, which means no units used and so is labelled 0. The *end* of the first unit indicates one unit used and so is marked 1; the end of each unit marks the number of units long the object is. These are complex ideas, but they must be developed if students are to use calibrated scales effectively. Making their own ruler or tape measure should assist students to understand how calibrated scales are made and used. They should also make their own calibrated scales for capacity, mass, angle and time.

Students who are through the Quantifying Phase can, given a practical unit of length, capacity or mass, use it to construct their own ruler, calibrated container or spring balance. Calibrated scales do not have to be in standard units, but it may be helpful for students to graduate their own measuring equipment in standard units before using purchased equipment. For example, a 2-metre height scale marked in centimetres and decimetres or a 10-metre string marked at 10-centimetre intervals can be prepared by the students themselves, as can calibrated containers.

Students should learn to read a range of graduated scales which progress in complexity from:

- every mark labelled; e.g. 1, 2, 3, … ; to

- some of the marks not labelled, but each mark is one unit; e.g. every fifth mark is labelled 5, 10, 15, 20 … ; to

- scales involving simple decimals; e.g. ten marks are placed between each whole but are not labelled; to

- the number of marks being fewer or greater than the number of units; e.g. every fifth mark is labelled 10, 20, 30, …, or every fifth mark is labelled 1, 2, 3, …

SAMPLE LEARNING ACTIVITIES

Beginning ✔✔

Straw Lengths

Have students each use one straw as a unit to measure paper strips that have been pre-cut to identical lengths. Compare any differences in results and talk about the various strategies used. Ask students to measure again, but this time have them mark the tape after each straw length to improve accuracy. Compare and discuss the consistency of the results. Ask: Why is it easier to check how many straws long it is when you mark each straw length as you go?

Stamps

Have students use the edge of an item (e.g. a matchbox, a block, an eraser, the end of a wooden ruler) to make 'stamp tapes' for measuring length. Invite them to stamp a row of the units along a paper strip, making sure they are just touching each other. Ask: Why do you need to be careful to have no gaps or overlaps if you are going to use the tape to measure how far you can jump? Organise students into groups and ask them to measure and describe lengths using their tapes (e.g. *I can jump nearly 30 matchbox stamps and just over 46 blocks*.)

Measuring Vertical Lengths

Ask: How could you use popsticks to measure vertical lengths like the height of the desk? (e.g. by gluing popsticks onto a strip of card) Lead students to the idea that popstick lengths can be marked on the card and numbered to save repeated lining up and counting, and have them make their own popstick tape measures from strips of paper. Invite students to use their tape measure to measure lengths in the classroom and compare results. Ask: What makes it easier to use the card than the popsticks? How do the numbers help?

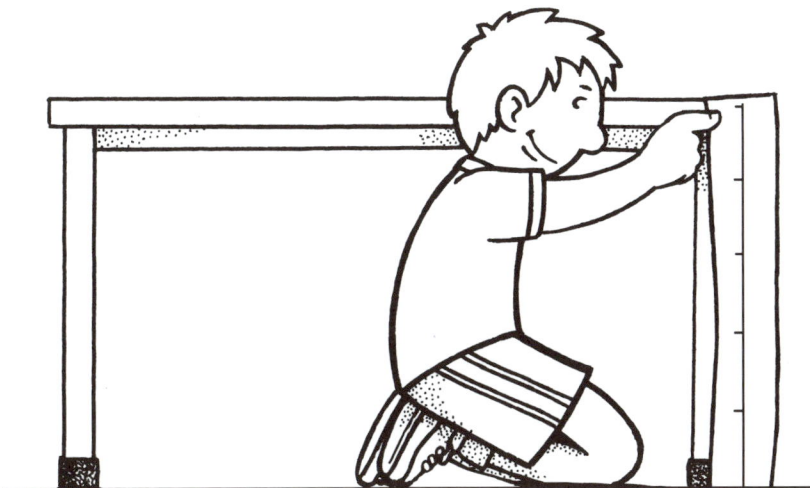

Make a Measuring Jug

Have students each make a measuring jug by cutting the top from a clear plastic bottle and calibrating it in 'cups'. Invite them to pour full cups of water into the jug, marking the level after each cupful. Encourage them to name the 'jugs' (e.g. the 2-cup jug). Ask students to use their jug to measure the capacity of containers, reading the scale. (e.g. *This jar holds a bit more than 3 cups*.)

Compare Measuring Jugs

As students use their own measuring jug in 'Make a Measuring Jug', focus on variations in the measures when two jugs have been made using the same cup. Ask: How could this happen? Invite students to watch each other make a new jug each and explain the variation. Encourage all students to recheck their use of units with a partner. Ask: Why might the marks not match when you put the two jugs together? How could the marks have ended up further apart on one of the jugs? What do you need to be very careful about when using the cup as your unit?

Calibrate Containers in Litres

Extend 'Make a Measuring Jug' and 'Compare Measuring Jugs' to calibrating larger containers in litres. For example, ask students to mark the inside of a bowl with a permanent marker after each litre is poured in. Compare the students' version with buckets and pans that are marked in litres on their internal surface. Ask: How are the markings different? How are they the same?

Comparing Spring Scales and Balance Scales

Ask students to place various packets or cans of food marked in gram weights (e.g. 200 grams, 250 grams, 500 grams) in opaque bags. Give groups of students different kitchen scales and spring scales and invite them to work out what the mass of the bag is and then to look in the bag to check their accuracy. Ask: How is the spring scale the same as the kitchen scale? How is it different?

SAMPLE LEARNING ACTIVITIES

Middle ✔✔✔

Measuring Height

Have students measure their height by lying down and placing MAB longs and small cubes along their length. Ask them to mark each piece used onto a strip of card and stick the strip to a wall or door. Invite students to measure and record their height in longs and small cubes again, this time using the marked scale on their vertical strip of card. Ask: Is there a difference in the two measurements? Why? Why not? What makes the vertical scale easier to use than the longs and cubes on the floor? (Link to Understand Units, Key Understanding 7.)

Using Different Tapes

Extend 'Measuring Height' by asking each student to measure their height using a different 'tape measure' (i.e. another student's strip of card marked in longs and small cubes). Ask: Are your measures the same amount? Why? Why not? Where the two tapes vary in accuracy, ask: If you measured yourself on your tape this month and then on someone else's tape next month, how would you know if you have grown? How can you check the tapes to make them all measure the same height in longs and small cubes?

Matchstick Tapes

Have students use an informal unit (e.g. popsticks, matchsticks) to construct a measuring tape, gluing multiple units onto a paper strip. Ask them to use this to measure each other and things around the classroom, including curves and awkward measurements. (e.g. length of their arm, waist measurement, circumference of the rubbish bin, height of desks, height of shelves). Discuss the advantages and disadvantages of using this type of tape measure. Have students then make a second tape by marking off the length of each popstick (matchstick). Invite them to decide where to put the numbers onto the tape. Draw out the conventional way to number the units from a zero starting point. Ask: What would happen if you wrote the number in the space rather than at the end of the unit? How is the second tape easier to use than the first? Encourage students to use their new tape to re-measure their objects. (See Sample Lesson 2, page 134.)

Varying Measurements

Extend 'Matchstick Tapes' by having pairs of students use their matchstick (popstick) tapes to measure the same set of objects. Ask: Why do the measurements vary? Will this happen if we use a ruler or a dressmaker's tape measure instead? How are these measuring tools the same as (different from) your matchstick (popstick) tapes?

Picture Frame

Ask students to use a ruler to measure around the edge of a picture in order to cut a length of card to frame it. Ask: Where do you start and finish each measurement? Which part of the ruler goes on the place that you start? How do you know how long each section is? Do the numbers label the lines or the spaces on the ruler? What do the numbers tell you? What do the small lines between the numbered lines mean? (See Understand Units, Key Understanding 4; link to Understand Units, Key Understanding 5.)

Nails and Elastic

Ask small groups of students to weigh ten nails by placing them into a bag on the end of a piece of elastic attached to the wall or pinup board. Have them mark the mass onto a strip of card taped up behind the 'scales', then weigh 20 nails (30 nails, 40 nails), mark the different positions on the card and use this calibrated scale to say how much other things weigh in 'nails' (e.g. the cup weighs the same as 20 nails). Ask: What makes the calibrated scale easier to use than balance scales? What if you lost the nails? Could you still use the balance scales to weigh in 'nails'? Could you still use your calibrated scale? What would you need to use if your object weighed much more than 40 nails? What would be the limits of your calibrated scale compared to the balance scale?

Broken Ruler

Have students use a paper representation of a broken piece of ruler with only the 6-centimetre to 10-centimetre section to measure several small items. Invite students to discuss the technique they used. Ask: Which part of the scale represents the centimetre lengths? (the spaces, not the marks). What would be the longest object we could measure without needing to move the ruler? What about if we included the millimetres?

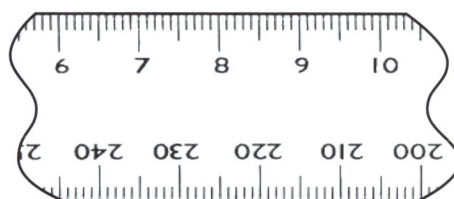

Middle ✔✔✔

Labelling Litres

Have students calibrate unmarked 10-litre plastic buckets in litres by pouring in 1-litre milk cartons of water and marking the level inside the bucket after each one. Discuss whether or not every litre mark needs to be numbered. Ask: What if we only labelled every five litres, how would you measure out 7 litres of water? (Link to Understand Units, Key Understanding 1 and Estimate, Key Understanding 2.)

Measuring Bottles

Ask students to make their own fluid measuring bottle from a plastic drink bottle using cupfuls as the unit and marking off the height of each one using an elastic band. Invite them to mark lines onto a paper strip to match the elastic bands, place the strip onto a different container and test whether they work for that container. Ask: Do the lines on the strip work for the new container? Why? Why not? What difference does it make if one of the bottles is wider than the other?

KU 4

SAMPLE LEARNING ACTIVITIES

Later ✔✔✔

Calibrating Containers

Have students make a container to measure small amounts of liquid. Show students a container calibrated every 250 millilitres. Ask: Can you tell me what these marks mean? Would it help you to accurately measure how much this small container holds? Why? Why not? Invite students to use materials (e.g. small cone medicine measurer, medicine spoon, ruler, disposable cups) to calibrate the container to make it a more suitable measuring tool. (See Understand Units, Key Understanding 5; link to Understand Units, Key Understanding 7.)

Angles

After comparing the size of angles directly (e.g. by placing the corner of a book on the corner of a desk to check they are the same angle, opening a compass to match how far the door is open), ask students to construct a cardboard 'protractor' using a paper plate. Have them fold their plate in half, then repeatedly in half to form 16 equal angles in the circle. Invite them to label the 'angle units' (i.e. the 16 equal sections of the circle) and use the instrument to measure and draw representations of angles of various numbers of 'angle units' (e.g. 15 angle units, 2 angle units). Ask: How can you label your protractor so that the turn can be measured in either direction? (Link to Indirect Measure, Key Understanding 4.)

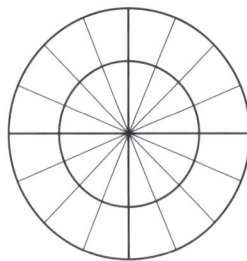

Two-Metre Tape

Have students construct a 2-metre measuring tape using MAB longs to calibrate the tape in metres (ten longs), in decimetres (one long) and centimetres (tenth of a long or small cube). Invite students to choose a labelling system to use on their tape. Ask: Is it necessary to label every marking? Where will you write the numbers for the decimetre lengths? What numbers will you write at the 1-metre and 2-metre markings? Invite pairs of students to measure various distances and circumferences, comparing the results obtained by their two tapes. Ask: Did you get the same measurement on each tape? Why? Why not? Why might your measurement differ? How can you check that your measuring tapes match each other?

Later ✔✔✔

Marks not Numbered

Have students read graduated scales where the marks are not all numbered. For example, give students measuring cups, jugs or cylinders and quantities of liquid to measure that will end up on the un-numbered calibrations. Ask: What do the marks between the numbers represent on your container? How do you know? How did you use the marks to work out how much water was in your container?

Reading Between the Lines

Extend 'Marks not Numbered' by having students attempt to measure out quantities of liquids that come between the marks on their measuring instrument. Ask: How do you know it is 325 millilitres when the beaker is calibrated every 100 millilitres? (e.g. *It's a quarter of the way up the space between the 300-millilitre and 400-millilitre marks and I know 25 is a quarter of 100, so it's 325 millilitres*.) How can you use your medicine cup to measure out 7 millilitres when there are no marks between 5 and 10 millilitres? Why does the cone shape of the medicine cup make it harder to judge the 'in between' measures accurately? (Link to Indirect Measure, Key Understanding 4.)

It Needs Fixing

Have students calculate to address inaccuracies in equipment. For example, say: Our tape measure has stretched so that when it says 1 metre, the object is really 1.2 centimetres longer. Ask: What would be the real length of a table that the stretched tape shows as a metre (the room that measures 4 metres, the chair that measures 50 centimetres, my desk that measures 1.5 cm)? After students have worked out their responses, invite them to work together to find a strategy for checking the correct lengths. For example, they might cut a length of paper tape 1.2 centimetres longer than a metre to use as a 'stretched' metre tape and measure out the incorrect lengths and then check them with a standard tape measure to find the true lengths. Ask: Does the stretched tape overestimate or underestimate the true length? (See Indirect Measure, Key Understanding 4.)

Slow Clock and Heavy Scales

Extend 'It Needs Fixing' by asking students to make adjustments for other calibrated scales. For example, say: Our clock is 5 minutes slow (fast). Ask: What should we do to work out what the right time is? Draw out that the situation requires addition (subtraction). Then, say: The bowl on the kitchen scales adds 100 grams to the weight. What should we do to work out the weight of what's in the bowl? Draw out that subtraction would be needed.

Calibrated Scales

Use an overhead projector to show a drawing of a measuring jug containing liquid. Place a scale on it, showing five calibrations between each whole number of litres. Ask students to record how much liquid there is. Then, remove the scale and replace it with one that has ten calibrations between each litre. Ask students again to record how much liquid there is. Some students are likely to have written different numbers (e.g. 1.3 for five gradations and 1.6 for ten gradations). Ask: Can both answers be right? Use the conflict between answers to generate discussion of the meaning of the gradations. Have students draw similar measuring jugs calibrated in different scales, then swap the drawings and show the liquid levels on the jugs. Have students swap again and work out the amount of liquid in litres. Ask: How did you work out the parts of a litre? Which scales were easiest to read? How can you be sure your reading is correct? (See *First Steps in Mathematics: Number*, Understand Numbers, Key Understanding 8.)

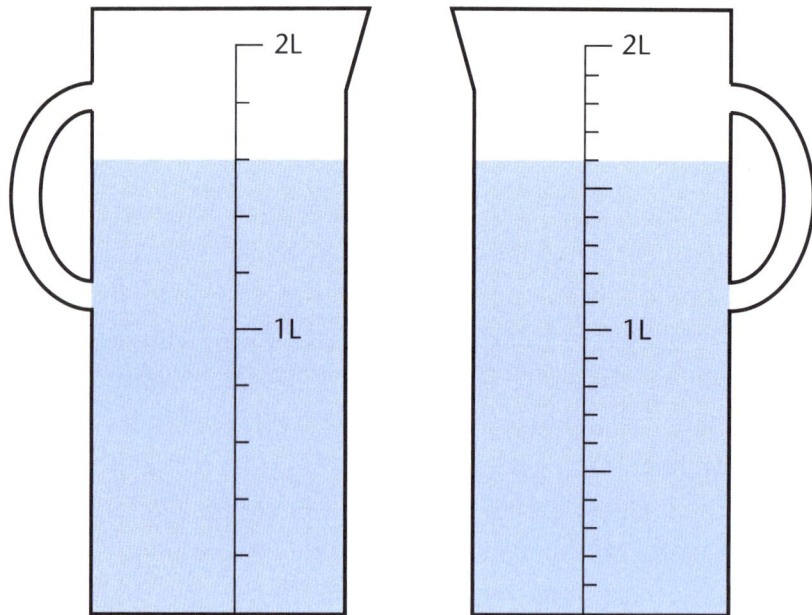

SAMPLE LESSON 2

Sample Learning Activity: Middle—'Matchstick Tapes', page 123

Key Understanding 4: Calibrated scales can be used as a substitute for repeating units when measuring length, capacity, mass, angle and time.

KU 4

Teacher's Purpose

My Year 4 students found the following drawing in an old maths book.

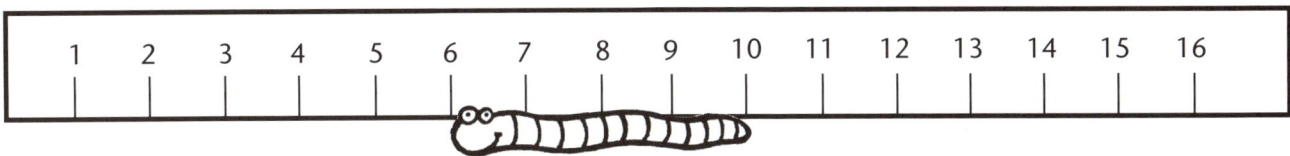

They all agreed it was 5 centimetres long! Probing revealed that the students were counting the marks, not the spaces between the marks. None thought to find the difference between 6 centimetres and 10 centimetres. They had not connected the calibrations on their rulers with the way we use physical units during length measuring activities. I decided I needed to help them make the link.

The probing questions included:

How did you work it out?

Show me what you counted.

Where did you start your count from?

Action and Reflection

I asked students to make a tape measure from paper tape using their own choice of a unit. I provided popsticks, straws, matchsticks, toothpicks, glue and paper tape.

They began gluing units along the tape, lining up their chosen units end-to-end without leaving spaces or overlaps. After a few minutes, Alex and Yenchee came and asked, 'Couldn't we just use a pen to mark where each popstick comes to?'

I was pleased to agree to this and thought it might be useful later in the lesson. When the tapes were dry, the students tried them out, measuring many objects in the room and around the school.

As a class, we then talked about the effectiveness of the measuring tapes. I was able to draw out the many disadvantages of having the actual units glued to the tape. Students made comments like, 'Using popsticks was good for straight things, but they wouldn't bend and the paper tore when we

Drawing out the disadvantages:

What problems did you have using your tape for measuring curved things?

Did you have the same problems when you were measuring straight things?

Did it matter that your popsticks fell off?

What did you do when your tape ripped?

Did that change the length of the popstick unit?

tried to measure around the tree' and 'Some of the matches fell off when we used ours.'

Then, Sharla said, 'It didn't really matter, because we could see where they'd been stuck on and we just counted where they'd been.'

This seemed the perfect opportunity to ask Alex and Yenchee to show how their tape was marked. Everyone thought this was much better than using the units themselves. I asked if anyone had difficulty counting the units as they were measuring.

Daniel said, 'Ours was matchsticks and Ben kept losing count, so, in the end, what we did was write the numbers next to the matchsticks so we didn't have to count.'

Several others had also done this, but I noticed that they had written the numbers next to the units.

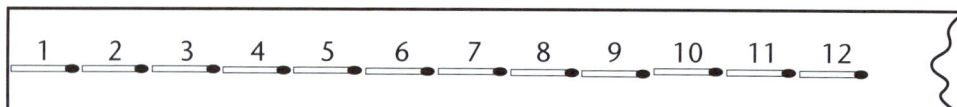

I decided that this needed to be the focus of my next lesson.

Connection and Challenge

The following day, I asked everyone to use what they'd found out and create a new 'improved' measuring tape using an agreed unit. We decided to make a 'matchstick measuring tape'. All took care to accurately mark the length of each matchstick on their tape, showing they had understood how the markings represented the units. When it came to numbering their scales, however, many wrote the numbers next to the space where the match had been, not close to the end marks. Several students had written '1' at the very beginning of the tape. There were a few who numbered their tapes in the conventional way.

Because I wanted to help students see for themselves how their unconventional markings could cause difficulties, I asked students in pairs to use their tapes to measure the same objects and talk about any differences they found. To maximise the chance for conflicting results, I purposely paired students who used different numbering methods.

This also helped me to see how individuals interpreted their own tape markings. I overheard Angie complain to Mohammed that he had written four where the three should be. Mohammed argued, 'But that's for that match, that four is for that match' (pointing to the fourth space).

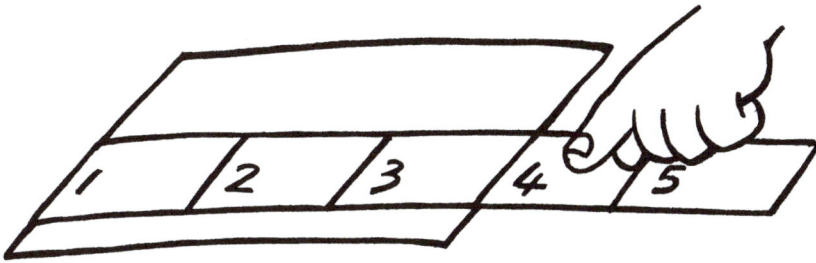

Angie was not satisfied and continued to insist it was misleading to do it that way. I called the class together at that stage and talked about everyone's experiences. I asked Angie to explain how her tape worked.

'I just line it up and look at the mark and the number is just there. See, it is three popsticks long.'

Drawing Out the Mathematical Idea

I asked other students to demonstrate how their tapes worked, including Mohammed. It soon became obvious to all the students that positioning the numbers at the right-hand end of each unit space (rather than within it or at the beginning of it) made it easier to keep track of the number of units and eventually everyone agreed this was the best strategy.

I was now confident that the students knew the value of marking off the length of their unit and using a number for each mark, but I wasn't sure that they had connected this with the way a standard ruler works. I decided that this would be the focus of tomorrow's lesson.

KU 4

> To facilitate the discussion I asked:
>
> *Show us how you used your tape to measure this book.*
>
> *How did you know how big the book is?*
>
> *Did the number help?*
>
> *If the end of the book was not on a mark, how did you know which matchstick to finish your count on?*
>
> *Can we say seven-and-a-half matchsticks long?*

? *Did You Know?*

A diagnostic activity for the middle and later years

Seven hundred students in upper primary and lower secondary schools were asked if they could tell how long the leaf is from the broken ruler. The illustration was accurate; that is, the distance between the centimetre marks was actually one centimetre on the diagram.

A small minority of students said 15 centimetres. Almost half in Year 5, one third in Year 6 and one quarter in Years 7 and 8 said the leaf was 7 centimetres long.

One wrote: *Starting from 9 cm (since it's a broken ruler), I counted 9 cm as 1 cm, 10 cm as 2 cm, 11 cm as …*

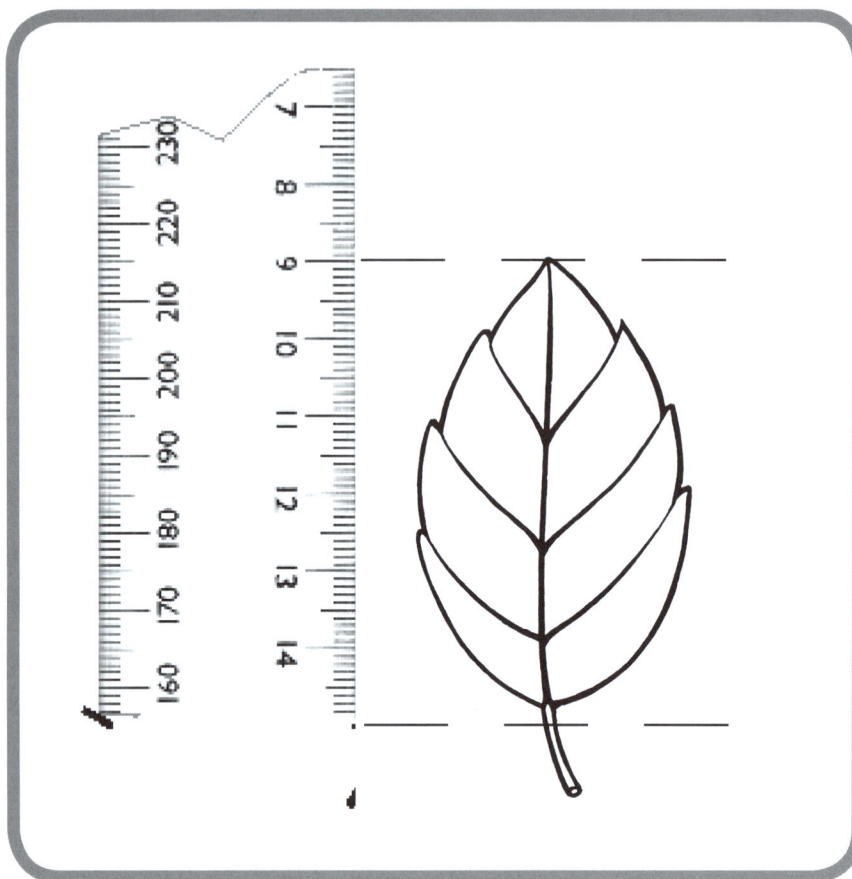

Another said: *You look at the 9 as a one and 15 is 7.*

Some even set up a table showing 9 = 1, 10 = 2, 11 = 3 and so on, to 'prove' their answer.

Most who correctly said 6 centimetres counted the centimetres or the spaces.

I got the answer by counting in between 9 and 10 and then 10 and 11 until I got to 14 and 15 and got the answer 6.

Very few were able to think of the 9 as a zero point or use the difference between 9 and 15 to find the length.

Many students experienced conflict, saying: *It could be 6 or it could be 7 depending on how you do it.*

For example, one Year 7 student came back to his teacher three times in the space of half an hour, asking to change his answer between 6 and 7. The conflict helped this student. Finally, he came back triumphantly and said: *It has to be 6 because you need to count 10 as 1, not the 9, 9 is just where the first centimetre starts.*

KEY UNDERSTANDING 5

Units are quantities and so we can use different representations of the same unit so long as we do not change the quantity.

As suggested in Key Understanding 3 in Understand Units, units are quantities; thus, 1 centimetre is an *amount* of length and 1 square metre is an *amount* of area. The same unit of area might be represented by a leaf, a triangular tile, or square grid paper. In classroom activities, however, we often refer informally to the object chosen to represent a unit as though it was itself the unit. Thus we talk about popsticks and hexagons as though they are units, when we really mean the length of the popstick or the area of the hexagon. When students use blocks as measuring instruments, for example, they may use the mass of the block as the unit for deciding how heavy something is, the length of its side for deciding how far away something is, and the area of a face for comparing the area of two leaves.

This distinction seems subtle, and the language needed to make it explicit is quite complex, so the informal way we refer to objects as though they are units is understandable, especially in the early years. Nevertheless, when we ask students to make sure that they choose a unit that will tile without gaps and overlaps, it is not surprising that they could think that two different shapes are two different units. If they have the same area, however, the two shapes are the *same* unit in different forms. Some *forms* are easier to use because they enable us to make a good match with the object to be measured (see Key Understanding 3). If students persist for too long with the idea that the particular objects or shapes are the units, then they may have difficulty progressing in their understanding of measurement.

For example, a length unit may be made from rubber and curved as needed; an area unit might be cut and rearranged. In order for students to make sense of this, they need to understand that units are really quantities and not objects. The form or look of the thing being used as a unit can change so long as it does not alter the relevant quantity. Students need to understand *why* a square metre can be cut to fit it into a shape when measuring area and a bit of play dough can be rolled and still be used as the same unit of mass, but not as the same unit of area. As indicated in the Background Notes on page 161, finding the area or volume of objects by direct measurement is more complex than finding length or capacity, both practically and conceptually, and needs careful development.

Students who are through the Quantifying Phase are able to use uniform units to measure quantities that are uni-dimensional, such as length, capacity and mass, as well as angle and time. They also use uniform units of area, although they may struggle with what to do along the edges when covering regions (see Key Understanding 3). While they may try to use some part-units of area, they may not be successful when it requires them to combine part-units.

Students who are through the Measuring Phase are able to use and combine part-units of area and can therefore count units and part-units to find the area of any region. They can also count units of volume in straightforward cases.

SAMPLE LEARNING ACTIVITIES

Beginning ✔

Pliable Units

Have students investigate situations where it helps to use pliable units such as pipe cleaners to measure length. Invite them to choose objects to use as units to measure lengths (e.g. distance around a ball, distance around a picture frame, distance around their shoe or footprint). Ask: What changes when you bend the pipe cleaner? What stays the same? How can you check that the bent pipe cleaner is just as long as the straight pipe cleaner? (Link to Understand Units, Key Understanding 3.)

KU 5

Trundle Wheel and Metre Rule

Ask students to compare the length around a trundle wheel to a metre rule. Use each to make a 2-metre chalk line on the playground and compare the two lines. Organise students into groups and ask some to use a metre rule and some to use a trundle wheel to measure the markings on the basketball court. Ask: What was easy (difficult) about using a metre rule? What was easy (difficult) about using a trundle wheel? What do you need to be careful about when using the trundle wheel? How did you keep track of where to begin the next metre when using the metre rule?

Play Dough Balls

Invite students to make play dough balls of equal size and use them to compare the capacity of margarine and yoghurt containers. Ask: How many balls fit into each container? Does it make a difference if you squash the balls to fit them in? Why do more fit in when you squash them up? Which container will fit the most balls? How do you know? What changed about the balls when you squashed them? What has stayed the same?

Covering the Desk

Ask students to find out how many whole pages of A4 paper fit onto their desks without any spaces between or overlaps at the edges. Ask: Are there any parts of the desk still not covered? If you cut up sheets of paper, how many more sheets do you think you would need to fill in the gaps? Invite them to take that number of extra sheets and cut them to fit one at a time to test how many they really need. Ask: How many pages altogether did you need to cover your desk? What changed and what stayed the same when you cut up pages to fit? (The shape changed, but the quantity of paper was the same.) (Link to Understand Units, Key Understanding 3.)

Leaves

Invite students to trace around a leaf and arrange whole 2-centimetre-squared tiles in ways that get the most into the area of the leaf. Ask: How could you fit another tile in? Will cutting it up help? Encourage students to keep track of how many tiles they have used with the fewest gaps, no overlaps and filled as close as possible to the edge of the outline of the leaf. Later, when students have become very careful about leaving no gaps or overlaps, draw attention to the way some have arranged tiles to make the job easier (e.g. rows and columns). (Link to Indirect Measure, Key Understanding 1.)

Bolts and Play Dough

Have students make collections of uniform units using different objects. For example, provide two bolts and a large ball of play dough for students to use as units to match the weight of objects that are heavier than two bolts. Ask: How can we use the play dough to make another thing to use that will be the same weight as a bolt? Encourage students to use the balance scales to make balls of play dough equal to a bolt.

Popsticks

Extend 'Bolts and Play Dough' by asking students to find objects equal in length to a popstick and make a collection of them to use as representations of the same unit. Ask: To find out how wide your desk is, would it matter if you started measuring with a popstick and then changed to one of the other objects? Why? Why not?